ANCHORS FOR THE SOUL

ANCHORS FOR THE SOUL

DENNIS L. LARGEY

Bookcraft
Salt Lake City, Utah

To my children

Gifford
Kobi
Zachary
Seth

Library of Congress Catalog Card Number: 88-64140
ISBN 0-88494-692-4

First Printing, 1989

Printed in the United States of America

Contents

	Acknowledgments	vii
	Introduction	1
1	Enduring to the End	5
2	Understanding Life's Purpose	10
3	Is It Worth It?	20
4	The Nature of the Opposition	26
5	The Power of Testimony	42
6	The Sustaining Vision	55
7	The Holy Ghost	62
8	Safeguards Called Commandments	74
9	Power Through Obedience	84
10	Decisions for Righteousness	95
11	God Is Faithful	101
12	Remember, Remember	108
13	The Purpose of the Church	113

14 Prayer, Scripture, Sacrament   120
15 Why Members Become Inactive   134
16 For Time and All Eternity   139
    References   143
    Index   147

Acknowledgments

I express my sincere appreciation to Robert W. Laird, Boyd O. Jarman, and Eric B. Shumway for the far-reaching effects they have had in my conversion to The Church of Jesus Christ of Latter-day Saints and in my personal life, and hence in the development of convictions and concepts that have made this book possible.

I express also my appreciation to my wife, Kristene, for her typing, proofreading, and insightful suggestions.

Introduction

Have you ever sat on the seashore and picked up a handful of sand and let it run slowly through your fingers? One evening I was sitting on a beautiful beach in Hawaii enjoying the sunset. After a while I developed a preoccupation with the sand—so many grains of sand! Billions of grains were within my sight and countless more extended down the numerous beaches.

Running the sand through my fingers I stopped to gaze at one singular grain. At that time I had a thought, the impact of which has never left me. If that one speck of sand represented the sixty or eighty years of earth life each of us expects to live, then what we do in that one grain of time will determine where we spend the remaining grains of time. What a motivating thought! All we have to do is keep the commandments and "endure to the end," and we will have an eternity in which to enjoy the rewards of eternal life.

When the prophet Nephi reached the end of his days, he wanted to make his last message so clear that his people could not possibly misunderstand his words. He defined plainly the "doctrine of Christ" and taught that obedience to the doctrine was the only way to gain salvation. The doctrine of Christ includes having faith in Jesus Christ, repenting of sin, being baptized, receiving the gift of the Holy Ghost, and enduring to the end in righteousness (see 2 Nephi 31).

We can be faithful for many years and yet lose salvation in the celestial kingdom if our righteousness does not extend to the end of our mortal life. The sons and daughters of God waited for perhaps eons of time in the premortal existence for the opportunity to come to earth. The scriptures are clear as to the purpose of life: we came to earth from another world for a very brief period, to be tested in regard to our faithfulness and devotion to the gospel of Jesus Christ. This faithfulness includes being active in the Church, obeying the commandments, giving heed to the prophets, showing faith during trial and adversity, and having our hearts centered on things pertaining to the kingdom of God. There is no second chance if our life does not measure up to the worthiness required for the destination we desire.

The path to eternal life can seem like an obstacle course. One time my wife and I were deliberating over a disturbing circumstance we were about to enter into. We felt that our decision was correct but feared the "rocks in the road" we knew would surface. One day Kristene said she had the answer to our dilemma. Her answer was simple but profound: "We know the pitfalls, and knowing the pitfalls can help us avoid them." The same is true in life and can be applied by members of the Church. Life is full of pitfalls which need to be dealt with. How we do this can make the difference in our spiritual success—forewarned is forearmed.

Athletes practice daily to perfect their skills. Coaches prepare them by simulating game situations in practice and providing the repetition to make the desired responses automatic. When the real moment in the real game comes the athlete reacts correctly because he has "seen it before." The coach has spoken about it in team meetings and the athletes have practiced it dozens of times.

The ideas presented in this book are derived from the scriptures. Hopefully the reader will receive from this book some coaching in regard to his personal quest to endure, for nothing is more important than passing the test of life.

1

Enduring to the End

Dictionary definitions of the term *endure* include: to remain firm under; to bear with patience.[1] Scripturally, to endure to the end means to follow the doctrine of Christ to the end of one's mortal life. The doctrine of Christ, as taught by Nephi, is that all men must have faith in Jesus Christ; repent of their sins; be baptized; and then receive the gift of the Holy Ghost. Obedience to this point places one on the path to eternal life.

Only the Beginning

Nephi explained, however, that one's work is only beginning after one has entered through the gate of repentance and baptism:

> And now, my beloved brethren, after ye have gotten into this strait and narrow path, I would ask if all is done? Behold, I say unto you, Nay; for ye have not come thus far save it were by the word of Christ with unshaken faith in him, relying wholly upon the merits of him who is mighty to save.

Wherefore, ye must press forward with a steadfastness in Christ, having a perfect brightness of hope, and a love of God and of all men. Wherefore, if ye shall press forward, feasting upon the word of Christ, and endure to the end, behold, thus saith the Father: Ye shall have eternal life.

And now, behold, my beloved brethren, *this is the way;* and there is none other way nor name given under heaven whereby man can be saved in the kingdom of God. And now, behold, this is the doctrine of Christ, and the only and true doctrine of the Father, and of the Son, and of the Holy Ghost, which is one God, without end. Amen. (2 Nephi 31:19–21; italics added.)

Enduring in righteousness to the end means sustained adherence to the four requirements cited in verse 20. Jesus' life epitomized these requirements, and his endurance to the end was crowned with the pronouncement, "It is finished; Father into thy hands I commend my spirit" (Luke 23:46; John 19:30). Exaltation in the celestial kingdom is earned through truly following the example set by Jesus Christ to the end of one's mortal life. He was perfect in his love, obedience, and sacrifice. We follow him imperfectly; however, this imperfection is counteracted through partaking of the infinite atonement, which enables the plan of mercy to save us.

Procrastination Is Dangerous

The scriptures plainly teach that "this life is the time for men to prepare to meet God" (Alma 34:32). In this context, the prophet Amulek encouraged his listeners to "not procrastinate the day of [their] repentance until the end; for after this day of life, which is given us to prepare for eternity, behold, if we do not improve our time while in this life, then cometh the night of darkness wherein there can be no labor performed" (Alma 34:33).

While teaching a Book of Mormon class at BYU, I was talking about the importance of repenting *now* because no one knows when he will die. A girl raised her hand and asked the question: "Is it possible to die on a bad day?" She then defined her question further by asking about the eternal situation of individuals who live most of their lives righteously yet fall into a short period of sinful living, during which time they die.

Her question made me think of a story about a friend of mine who, shortly after his conversion, became inactive in the Church. He and a few companions went out drinking and became very intoxicated. They stopped at a railway crossing that was flashing the warning of an oncoming train. The driver suggested that they ignore the sign, proceed over the tracks, and try to beat the train. At that moment a car rear-ended them and knocked their car onto the tracks. Both doors jammed, and although the driver reved the engine the car would not go forward. My friend remembered looking out the window and seeing the train heading directly for him. Sparks flew as the wheels of the train locked on the tracks in an effort to stop. Instantly he thought to himself, "Oh no! I'll be standing before my Maker drunk!" At the last second the driver discovered that the car wouldn't go because the impact of the collision had knocked the gears into neutral. He slammed the car into first gear and sped off the tracks. This incident became a turning point in my friend's life; a time when he reflected upon his situation and decided it was time to go back to church. He became very grateful for *another day* to prepare to meet God.

Inasmuch as most of us do not know when the "night of darkness," or death, will come to us, we are gambling with our own souls when we spend time away from God and his church. In answer to my student's question: Although it is not intentional, people can and do die during times of spiritual failure.

Walking in the Strait Path

There are numerous scriptural passages which teach the necessity of and blessings from enduring in righteousness to the end.

Nephi wrote concerning latter-day Gentiles: "I also have charity for the Gentiles. But behold, for none of these can I hope except they shall be reconciled unto Christ, and enter into the narrow gate, and walk in the strait path which leads to life, and continue in the path until the end of the day of probation." (2 Nephi 33:9.)

In this verse Nephi is giving a three-fold formula to achieve salvation: to *enter*, to *walk*, and to *continue*. Entrance through the gate of repentance and baptism, and even an extended walk on the straight path, is not enough to bring the necessary reconciliation with Christ if one fails to "continue . . . until the end." One could not expect to arrive at the seaside if one stopped in the desert, no matter how long it took to get to the desert. The destination is fixed and the mileage is already determined. Similarly, if life is a journey to the celestial kingdom, death becomes everyone's point of arrival, and righteousness assures the necessary distance.

There is an "if" clause in the doctrine of Christ. To the twelve Nephite disciples Jesus said: "whoso repenteth and is baptized in my name shall be filled; and *if* he endureth to the end, behold, him will I hold guiltless before my Father" (3 Nephi 27:16; italics added). The Lord told Joseph Smith and Oliver Cowdery: "*If* thou wilt do good, yea, and hold out faithful to the end, thou shalt be saved in the kingdom of God" (D&C 6:13; italics added).

Perhaps if there were to be a "fifth first principle" of the gospel it would be to endure to the end. Righteousness must persist to the end of our mortal lives if we are to receive the full measure of eternal glory. Considering the truth of this doctrine, it would seem a great and foolish error to neglect to form a plan that would sustain us when we are faced with temptation, trial, boredom, apathy, or just plain "tiredness" as we seek to stay active in the Church and righteous in our lives. If a man were to receive a million dollars if he would stop smoking for one week, would he not make detailed plans that covered every minute of every day for the entire week? He would intellectually study out the problem he faced and preplan his behavior as to what he would do when confronted with any opposition to his obtaining the desired reward.

We might think it foolish to consider one week for a million dollars. Think of sixty to eighty years for eternal life—the greatest of all God's gifts! If we could somehow comprehend the duration of eternity, the sixty or eighty years of mortality would be just a blink of an eye—hardly even noticeable—not even comparable to the week's challenge for the million dollars. It is a matter of perspective. Earth life is so very short, yet the consequences of our obedience or disobedience determines the unalterable bounds of our residence for eternity.

2

Understanding Life's Purpose

Over the years in the religion classes I have taught, I have asked students to raise their hands if they are new converts to the Church. I then ask them: "What became a part of your life after you found the gospel that you did not have before?" The most common first response has always been, "A purpose in life."

A well-known fact of life is that we are more likely to persist in a task if we have a clear understanding of the purpose of it. Knowing "why" can often make a big difference in our ability to persevere. Scientists endure long hours of research and testing because they know the possible consequences to mankind of their successful experiments. Effective soldiers have a cause which fuels their determination to win on the battlefield. Throughout history, when freedom was the objective of conflict, heroes emerged on every front; people become great when great causes burn within.

Persistence in the gospel cause until the required end necessitates an understanding of the purposes of God. According to Nephi, Laman and Lemuel murmured because "they knew not the dealings of that God who had created them" (1 Nephi 2:12). Central to our understanding of life's purpose is an understanding of Jesus Christ: "For this is life eternal, that they might know thee the only true God, and Jesus Christ, whom thou hast sent" (John 17:3). Jesus is the champion of the gospel cause. His life exemplified, or marked, the path disciples must follow. The Atonement made eternal progression possible. The plan of God for the salvation of his children was made operational because Jesus did not shrink from drinking the bitter cup in the offering of himself as a sacrifice for sin.

Probationary Nature of Our Existence

Anciently, the Lord showed Abraham a great vision. The revelation clearly identified the purpose of our mortal existence upon the earth.

> Now the Lord had shown unto me, Abraham, the intelligences that were organized before the world was; and among all these there were many of the noble and great ones;
>
> And God saw these souls that they were good, and he stood in the midst of them, and he said: These I will make my rulers; for he stood among those that were spirits, and he saw that they were good; and he said unto me: Abraham, thou art one of them; thou wast chosen before thou wast born.
>
> And there stood one among them that was like unto God, and he said unto those who were with him: We will go down, for there is space there, and we will take of these materials, and we will make an earth whereon these may dwell;
>
> And we will prove them herewith, to see if they will do all things whatsoever the Lord their God shall command them;
>
> And they who keep their first estate shall be added upon; and they who keep not their first estate shall not have glory in the same kingdom with those who keep their

first estate; and they who keep their second estate shall have glory added upon their heads forever and ever. (Abraham 3:22–26.)

Our first estate was our premortal existence. By accepting Christ and the plan of salvation laid down by the Father, we "kept" our first estate and thus progressed into our second estate. We were "added upon" at this point, having gained a physical body and the opportunities of mortality. Consequently, to have glory added upon our heads forever we must keep our second estate. Success in the second estate necessitates proving ourselves, or, as the scriptures state, "[doing] all things whatsoever the Lord [our] God shall command [us]" (Abraham 3:25). This is the purpose of life. We evolve from one state to another, as part of a divine plan of eternal progression.

There Must Be Opposition

Lehi, speaking to his son Jacob, taught that "it must needs be, that there is an opposition in all things. If not so, . . . righteousness could not be brought to pass, neither wickedness, neither holiness nor misery, neither good nor bad." Lehi said that without this opposition there would have been no purpose in the end of creation. God created both things to act and things to be acted upon, and man could not act for himself save he should be "enticed by the one or the other." (2 Nephi 2:11, 12, 13, 14, 16.)

The transgression of Adam and Eve in the Garden of Eden set in place the conditions wherein mankind could, as was shown to Abraham, prove himself before God. With Adam's fall came the availability of choices. One choice, without any opposition, is really not a choice at all; opposites, good and evil, make it possible to be tested.

Lehi further taught that after Adam and Eve were driven out of the Garden of Eden "the days of the children of men were prolonged, according to the will of God, that they might repent while in the flesh; wherefore, their state became a *state of probation*, and their time was lengthened, according to the commandments which the Lord God gave unto the children of men'' (2 Nephi 2:21; italics added).

Alma also spoke of mortality as a probationary experience: ''And we see that death comes upon mankind, yea, the death which has been spoken of by Amulek, which is the temporal death; nevertheless there was a space granted unto man in which he might repent; therefore this life became a probationary state; a time to prepare to meet God; a time to prepare for that endless state which has been spoken of by us, which is after the resurrection of the dead'' (Alma 12:24).

If, then, life is a probationary experience, by the very nature of this descriptive clause we should expect periods of soul-testing; times which are not easy. Brigham Young taught:

> We are now in a day of trial to prove ourselves worthy or unworthy of the life which is to come. . . .
>
> The people of the most high God must be tried. It is written that they will be tried in all things, even as Abraham was tried. If we are called to go upon Mount Moriah to sacrifice a few of our Isaacs, it is no matter; we may just as well do that as anything else. I think there is a prospect for the Saints to have all the trials they wish for, or can desire.
>
> All intelligent beings who are crowned with crowns of glory, immortality, and eternal lives, must pass through every ordeal appointed for intelligent beings to pass through to gain their glory and exaltation. Every calamity that can come upon mortal beings will be suffered to come upon the few, to prepare them to enjoy the presence of the Lord. If we obtain the glory that Abraham obtained, we must do so by the same means that he did. If we are ever prepared to enjoy the society of Enoch, Noah, Melchizedek, Abraham, Isaac, and Jacob, or of their faithful children, and of the faithful Prophets and Apostles, we must pass through the same experience, and gain the knowl-

edge, intelligence, and endowments that will prepare us to enter the celestial kingdom of our father and God. How many of the Latter-day Saints will endure all these things, and be prepared to enjoy the presence of the Father and the Son? You can answer that question at your leisure. Every trial and experience you have passed through is necessary for your salvation.[1]

Wise teachers teach students principles and then test them by posing hypothetical situations which require them to select which principle applies to a given situation. The Church teaches gospel principles with plainness. Everyday life provides the situations to which we, as children and pupils, make applications. Enough right principles applied to the many and varied circumstances of life will earn the Lord's recognition, "Well done, thou good and faithful servant: thou hast been faithful over a few things, I will make thee ruler over many things" (Matthew 25:21).

Understanding the probationary status of life provides a wide-range perspective which enables faith in Jesus Christ to conquer the problems and difficulties that come our way.

Purpose in Problems

Everyone faces problems and difficulties. Some are of our own making, while others enter our lives quite unexpectedly and through no fault of our own. Heavenly Father's plan requires that life's terrain be challenging. "I will prove them herewith," he told Abraham (Abraham 3:25). How could he prove his children without providing rocks, hills, mountains, thorns, thistles, and noxious weeds? Smooth and flat roads require for less strain and perspiration. Obstacles tighten muscles and harden bodies. Without the trial of our virtues, our character is not strengthened. This is not acceptable to our Heavenly Father. Elder Neal Maxwell said in a sermon: "God is a tutorial activist who loves His children too much to let us go on being just what we now are, because He knows what we have the power to become."[2]

I have often reflected on the things a friend said to me after he had given me a blessing. I had undergone some setbacks and felt unable to understand my situation and make the necessary decisions that were required of me. After taking his hands from my head, he looked at me soberly, and said, "Dennis, you haven't been in Liberty Jail six months yet. The Lord never promised a life of ease and comfort. He did promise us experience."

He was referring to the Prophet Joseph Smith's incarceration in Liberty Jail when the Prophet needed the Lord's assurance. The Lord responded to his plea, recognizing the persecution Joseph was required to endure, by saying:

> And if thou shouldst be cast into the pit, or into the hands of murderers, and the sentence of death passed upon thee; if thou be cast into the deep; if the billowing surge conspire against thee; if fierce winds become thine enemy; if the heavens gather blackness, and all the elements combine to hedge up the way; and above all, if the very jaws of hell shall gape open the mouth wide after thee, know thou, my son, that all these things shall give thee *experience*, and shall be for thy good.
>
> The Son of Man hath descended below them all. Art thou greater than he? (D&C 122:7–8; italics added.)

I realized that good would ultimately come from my present trials, and that I would gain invaluable experience that would somehow be of help in my future life, if I "endured it well." Eventually answers did come, and the decisions that needed to be made became clear to me.

The Creation, the Fall, and the Atonement

Eternal progression required the creation of the earth, the fall of Adam, and the atonement of Jesus Christ. Each of the three events are related, and each depends on the other. One without the other is useless — all three events together are central to the operation of the plan of salvation.

As spirit sons and daughters of God we lived with our Heavenly Father in a premortal life. As children we had a desire to be like him. As we could see that he had a perfected body of flesh and bones, the only way to progress to become like him was to leave the world of spirits and go to a "school," which would make available the conditions wherein godlike growth could result. The earth, therefore, was created to serve as a school wherein each of God's children could work out his salvation.

After the creation of the school, or this earth, there had to be a way to get there. The fall of Adam was the vehicle which enabled us to come to earth. The Fall was necessary not only because it made it possible for us to come to earth —"for Adam fell that men might be" (2 Nephi 2:25)—but also because it initiated certain conditions necessary for our growth. Mortality and physical death came into the world. Each of us could now work and live in a setting of opposition, with opportunity to select good over evil, thus *deliberately* becoming righteous.

Another consequence of Adam's transgression was spiritual death. This does not mean that our spirits literally die, but that we are separated from God's presence; a condition necessary if life is truly to be a testing period. We needed a school where we could learn to walk by faith, not by sight.

At the end of our schooling experience, a vehicle to carry us home was required. The way home for all of God's children is the atonement of Jesus Christ. The Atonement cancels the consequences of Adam's transgression: "For as in Adam all die, even so in Christ shall all be made alive" (1 Corinthians 15:22). This is universal; everyone will be resurrected and regain God's presence, there to be judged according to their works. Because of the atonement of Jesus Christ everyone has a guaranteed partial "ride home." The physical death brought about by Adam's transgression was overcome by the Resurrection, and the spiritual death was overcome for the righteous by Christ's atoning sacrifice, allowing them to return to their heavenly home. Thus when we stand in God's presence on Judgment Day we will be judged according to what we did during mortality. What we did while in this school, therefore, will determine where we will live after this school is out.

Heaven is a place of cleanliness and no unclean thing can dwell therein (1 Nephi 15:34). Not one person who ever dwelt upon the earth, save Jesus Christ, was perfect or will attain perfection during mortality. Therefore, everyone needs the power of the Atonement to redeem himself not only from the consequences of Adam's fall but also from his own errors. If we have applied the atonement of Jesus Christ by having a broken heart and a contrite spirit, living in obedience to the laws and ordinances of the gospel, and enduring to the end, we will qualify for eternal life.

Without the Creation, there would be no school; without the Fall, no mortality; without the Atonement, no eternal life. Jacob identified the consequences for mankind had there been no atonement:

> For as death hath passed upon all men, to fulfil the merciful plan of the great Creator, there must needs be a power of resurrection, and the resurrection must needs come unto man by reason of the fall; and the fall came by reason of transgression; and because man became fallen they were cut off from the presence of the Lord.
>
> Wherefore, it must needs be an infinite atonement— save it should be an infinite atonement this corruption could not put on incorruption. Wherefore, the first judgment which came upon man must needs have remained to an endless duration. And if so, this flesh must have laid down to rot and to crumble to its mother earth, to rise no more.
>
> O the wisdom of God, his mercy and grace! For behold, if the flesh should rise no more our spirits must become subject to that angel who fell from before the pres-

ence of the Eternal God, and became the devil, to rise no
more.

And our spirits must have become like unto him, and
we become devils, angels to a devil, to be shut out from
the presence of our God, and to remain with the father of
lies, in misery, like unto himself; yea, to that being who
beguiled our first parents, who transformeth himself nigh
unto an angel of light, and stirreth up the children of men
unto secret combinations of murder and all manner of secret works of darkness. (2 Nephi 9:6–9.)

Assurance and Security

To know with a surety where we came from, why we
are here, and where we are going when we leave this life
gives us security in our persistence. We came from somewhere and we are going somewhere—we can look forward
to the arrival, but we can also enjoy the journey. The Creation was no happenstance. God created an earth for his
children to enable them to progress and obtain a fulness of
eternal opportunity. It is natural for good parents to desire
the best for their children; consequently, they provide the
circumstances to achieve success. Students know that
school requires work and testing. Teachers and textbooks
provide all that is necessary to pass any of the scheduled
exams. Would a master teacher fail to provide information
or needed support to enable a student to pass his class?

Heavenly Father has given us all we need to qualify to
live in his kingdom. Bound up in this bundle of support
and instruction we have prophets, priesthood, and scriptures. We have been given a divine church administering
the ordinances of salvation. Above all, we have the testament of God's love through the sacrifice of his beloved
Son. "For God so loved the world, that he gave his only
begotten Son, that whosoever believeth in him should not
perish, but have everlasting life" (John 3:16). With this
knowledge, what else really matters? What the Lord said

to Joseph Smith and Oliver Cowdery is applicable to all of us: "Look unto me in every thought; doubt not, fear not. Behold the wounds which pierced my side, and also the prints of the nails in my hands and feet; be faithful, keep my commandments, and ye shall inherit the kingdom of heaven." (D&C 6:36–37.)

3

Is It Worth It?

To what end are we seeking to endure? What is heaven like? The Apostle Paul described this weight of eternal glory by saying: "Eye hath not seen, nor ear heard, neither have entered into the heart of man, the things which God hath prepared for them that love him" (1 Corinthians 2:9). In the Doctrine and Covenants we read: "And, if you keep my commandments and endure to the end you shall have eternal life, which gift is the greatest of all the gifts of God" (D&C 14:7). We often hear about the wisdom of selective and spaced gift-giving to our children. This is wise so as not to "spoil" the child. However, the bestowal of gifts to obedient children in the hereafter will be unrestricted. The Father will not be concerned about giving "too much," for he will give all that he has. "And he that receiveth my Father receiveth my Father's kingdom; therefore all that my Father hath shall be given unto him" (D&C 84:38).

The scriptures give us a partial idea of what awaits the faithful. On 21 January 1836, Joseph Smith, while in the Kirtland Temple, had the following vision:

The heavens were opened upon us, and I beheld the celestial kingdom of God, and the glory thereof, whether in the body or out I cannot tell.

I saw the transcendent beauty of the gate through which the heirs of that kingdom will enter, which was like unto circling flames of fire;

Also the blazing throne of God, whereon was seated the Father and the Son.

I saw the beautiful streets of that kingdom, which had the appearance of being paved with gold. (D&C 137:1–4.)

The heirs of salvation, those who will pass through the transcendent gate and walk the beautiful streets, are those who have proven their righteousness over a lifetime of mortal experience. Consequently, all others must dwell elsewhere, being judged "according to their works, and every man shall receive according to his own works, his own dominion, in the mansions which are prepared; . . . but where God and Christ dwell they cannot come, worlds without end" (D&C 76:111–12).

What We Forfeit If We Fail to Endure

Wise decision-making includes weighing the alternatives and considering the consequences of each option. Whether we achieve the kingdom of God or not is based on personal choice and our continuing ability to live consistently with our choices. If we are driving to Montana to see our relatives and we stop in Arizona and stay, that is our decision. Even if the car should break down or the money should run out, cars can be fixed and jobs can be obtained. If, however, we decide to stay in Arizona, we receive the consequences of not going to Montana. If the benefits of staying in Arizona outweigh the consequences of not going to Montana, there is no sadness in not obtaining the original goal. Similarly with our journey through this life.

Perhaps too few of us carefully consider what we would be forfeiting by beginning the journey toward the celestial kingdom and then getting sidetracked permanently along the way. It is a more positive venture to list what we would gain by enduring to the end; however, it is perhaps more sobering to see clearly what we lose by failing to "press forward." The following list represents what is willfully given up when choosing not to stay on course:

1. *Exaltation.* Exaltation is eternal life in the presence of God the Father and Jesus Christ forever and ever (see D&C 76:62).

2. *Never-ending happiness.* In his last sermon, King Benjamin said to his people:

> And moreover, I would desire that ye should consider on the blessed and happy state of those that keep the commandments of God. For behold, they are blessed in all things, both temporal and spiritual; and if they hold out faithful to the end they are received into heaven, that thereby they may dwell with God in a state of never-ending happiness. . . . (Mosiah 2:41.)

3. *Eternal marriage.* The scriptures make it clear that only those who receive exaltation will enjoy the continuance of their marriage relationship.

> In the celestial glory there are three heavens or degrees;
> And in order to obtain the highest, a man must enter into this order of the priesthood [meaning the new and everlasting covenant of marriage];
> And if he does not, he cannot obtain it.
> He may enter into the other, but that is the end of his kingdom; he cannot have an increase. (D&C 131:1–4.)

4. *Eternal increase and godhood.* Failure to obtain the highest degree in the celestial kingdom is failure to achieve the full measure of one's existence. Our potential is to become like our heavenly parents. Enduring to the end in righteousness in mortality qualifies us to go on to our eventual perfection. By obtaining godhood each of us, along with his or her eternal companion, will be able to partici-

pate in God's continuing plan through the powers of pro-creation. In section 132 of the Doctrine and Covenants we read:

> And again, verily I say unto you, if a man marry a wife by my word, which is my law, and by the new and everlasting covenant, and it is sealed unto them by the Holy Spirit of promise . . . it shall be done unto them in all things whatsoever my servant hath put upon them, in time, and through all eternity; and shall be of full force when they are out of the world; and they shall pass by the angels, and the gods, which are set there, to their exalta-tion and glory in all things, as hath been sealed upon their heads, which glory shall be a fulness and a *continuation of the seeds forever and ever.*
>
> Then shall they be gods, because they have no end; therefore shall they be from everlasting to everlasting, be-cause they continue; then shall they be above all, because all things are subject unto them. Then shall they be gods, because they have all power, and the angels are subject unto them.
>
> Verily, verily, I say unto you, except ye abide my law ye cannot attain to this glory. (D&C 132:19–21; italics added.)

5. *The first resurrection.* The morning of the first res-urrection is reserved for those who have kept their cove-nants. At the Waters of Mormon, Alma listed the covenants his people would be required to take upon themselves at baptism, and then gave promises to those who would remain faithful, "even until death:"

> And it came to pass that he [Alma] said unto them: Be-hold, here are the waters of Mormon . . . and now, as ye are desirous to come into the fold of God, and to be called his people, and are willing to bear one another's burdens, that they may be light;
>
> Yea, and are willing to mourn with those that mourn; yea, and comfort those that stand in need of comfort, and to stand as witnesses of God at all times and in all things,

and in all places . . . that ye may be redeemed of God, and be numbered with those of the first resurrection that ye may have eternal life. (Mosiah 18:8-9.)

6. *Being joint heirs with Jesus Christ (see Romans 8:16-17)*. Jesus, the Firstborn, is heir to all the treasures of our Father in Heaven's kingdom. The righteous are promised the same, and thus they become joint heirs. This inheritance includes "thrones, kingdoms, principalities, and powers, dominions, all heights and depths." (D&C 132:19.)

7. *A celestial body*. Obedience to celestial law qualifies one to receive a celestial body, which can abide the glory found in the celestial kingdom (see D&C 88:19-29). "These are they whose bodies are celestial, whose glory is that of the sun, even the glory of God, the highest of all, whose glory the sun of the firmament is written of as being typical" (D&C 76:70).

In a general conference address, Elder Sterling W. Sill contrasted the physical body with the celestial body promised to the faithful:

> We all know the things that we do to make this body a pleasant habitation. We bathe it and keep it clean; we dress it in the most appropriate clothing. Sometimes we ornament it with jewelry. If we're very wealthy we buy necklaces and bracelets and diamond rings and other things to make this body sparkle and shine and make it a pleasant place. . . .
>
> Now if you think it would be pleasant to be dressed in expensive clothing, what do you think it would be like sometime to be dressed in an expensive body—one that shines like the sun, one that is beautiful beyond all comprehension, with quickened senses, amplified powers of perception, and vastly increased capacity for love, understanding, and happiness.[1]

In essence, those who are to be rewarded with eternal life come forth in the first resurrection with celestial bodies. They dwell forever with the Father and Jesus Christ in a never-ending state of happiness. They continue in family relationships, and as joint heirs with Jesus Christ they receive "all that the Father hath."

Heaven: Is it worth it? If one honestly ponders over the preceding list, how could one desire anything else? Why would one want to be en route to the celestial kingdom and then end up in a kingdom of lesser glory? As in the example of the driver traveling to Montana who instead stops permanently in Arizona, the choice is ours. It is essential to count the cost of discipleship and weigh the consequences of the direction our life is taking. There is too much to lose for us to take lightly the message of the gospel of Jesus Christ.

4

The Nature of the Opposition

In a letter to his son Moroni, Mormon wrote: "We have a labor to perform whilst in this tabernacle of clay, that we may conquer the enemy of all righteousness, and rest our souls in the kingdom of God" (Moroni 9:6). The enemy of all righteousness is Satan. He is real; he seeks the downfall of all of God's children. Satan lost his own salvation (see Moses 4:1–4), and now desires "that all men might be miserable like unto himself" (2 Nephi 2:27).

Satan's opportunities to interfere with a person's celestial achievement begin at baptism and continue until death. His goal is to "[persuade] men to do evil, . . . believe not in Christ, . . . deny him, and serve not God" (Moroni 7:17).

Satan's Strategies Can Be Known

Several years ago two professional football teams met in an important playoff game. The odds were in favor of one particular team. During the contest, the team that was supposed to lose intercepted two key passes and returned the ball each time for a touchdown. After the upset victory it was discovered that an assistant coach, with the aid of binoculars, had decoded the signals being sent to the quarterback indicating the primary receiver. With the aid of a walkie-talkie, the assistant had relayed the information to the defensive backfield coach, who had then informed his players on the field through substitution. Knowing the specific plans of the opposition had enabled the defense to become the offense and effect the victory.

Today, teams go to great effort to protect their game plans. Practice sessions are closed, fences are covered to prevent observation, decoys are used when sending in signals, and players are heavily fined for the loss of a playbook. In the above example the method the assistant coach used to obtain an advantage was, of course, against fair play. The story illustrates, however, the obvious fact that knowing the strategy of an adversary gives one an advantage.

Satan, "the father of all lies," is a master of deception. Knowing his strategies, Heavenly Father has righteously opened to his children, through the Book of Mormon, Satan's unholy playbook. We can therefore know his strategy and counteract his effort. In the April 1975 general conference of The Church of Jesus Christ of Latter-day Saints, President Ezra Taft Benson, speaking about the Book of Mormon, said: "Is the Book of Mormon true? Yes. Who is it for? Us. What is its purpose? To bring men to Christ. How does it do this? By testifying of Christ and revealing his enemies."[1]

In Nephi's writings, several of Satan's deceptions are revealed.

> For behold, at that day shall he rage in the hearts of the children of men, and stir them up to anger against that which is good.
> And others will he pacify, and lull them away into carnal security, that they will say: All is well in Zion; yea,

Zion prospereth, all is well—and thus the devil cheateth
their souls, and leadeth them away carefully down to hell.

And behold, others he flattereth away, and telleth them
there is no hell; and he sayeth unto them: I am no devil,
for there is none—and thus he whispereth in their ears,
until he grasps them with his awful chains, from whence
there is no deliverance. (2 Nephi 28:20–22.)

An examination of some key words used in this passage
is helpful to broaden one's understanding of how Satan operates: First he *pacifies,* which means to appease or pla-
cate. Second he *cheats,* which means to deceive by trick-
ery; to swindle, to mislead; to fool; or to practice fraud.
Third he *flatters,* which means to compliment excessively
and often insincerely, especially in order to win the favor
of; to feed the vanity of; or to persuade that something one
wants to believe is the case. Fourth he *leads,* which means
to show the way by going in advance; to conduct, escort, or
direct; to cause to follow some course of action or line of
thought. All of this—the pacifying, the cheating, the flattery, and the leading,—is done *carefully,* which is synony-
mous with thoroughly; painstakingly; and conscien-
tiously.[2]

Satan thus customizes his dishonesty according to the
susceptibility of his target. His favorite approach is "whatever works." In the pride of his heart he does not drive
from the rear but leads from the front. Knowing only a few
would follow him if his true identity and design were man-
ifested, he carefully draws people into the false conclusion
of supposing they are winning when in fact they are
slowly, but nevertheless effectively, being destroyed.

Some individuals Satan stirs to anger against that
which is good. Many people are stirred to anger against the
work of the Restoration and particularly against the Book
of Mormon. This anger blinds their eyes and closes their
hearts to its message. Satan of course is pleased. It does
not matter to him if people denounce him and proclaim

Christ, if, in their religious creeds, they are blindly riveted to false doctrine and the traditions of men.

While verse 20 describes the work of an enemy outside the Church, verse 21 identifies an enemy within the Church—apathy.

Many parents express gratitude for the invention of the pacifier. Fix the pacifier in the baby's mouth and as the sucking motion intensifies the eyes begin to shut. Satan pacifies those in Zion who have the propensity to relax in their discipleship, causing them to believe that "all is well." When people become too secure in their righteousness they can develop a blind side in their own spirituality. This opens the door for Satan to lead them carefully, and almost imperceptibly, away from the spiritual nourishment that comes from "being alive in Christ." A quick pace turns to a lethargic plod, and the member is no longer a watchful disciple. As did the goodman of the house, he "falls asleep," and the property (in this case, his soul) is open for the thief to come in and plunder (see Matthew 24:43).

How is it that some who dwell in Zion in an apathetic state are able to say "All is well?" Perhaps it is because some allow the world to become their standard in matters of personal righteousness. In their pacified condition, although not in stride yet nevertheless on the same track and going in the same direction, these Saints are slowly moving with the times instead of being fastened securely to the rock. By following the world they are slowly being choked by the tares and pierced by the thorns of worldly measures. For example, the standard of acceptance of certain material presented on the movie screen has degenerated until today, without any measured reaction, some people view films which would have been shocking to them a few years previous. Should parents in Zion allow the world, with its steady decline in moral values, to decide what is acceptable and what is not? At what age can certain film

content be viewed through the various rating designations
now in use? The Lord said: "Behold, I, the Lord, have
made my church in these last days like unto a judge sitting
on a hill, or in a high place, to judge the nations. For it
shall come to pass that the inhabitants of Zion shall judge
all things pertaining to Zion." (D&C 64:37–38.) True spiritual health comes through a continual upward reach toward obedience to laws, principles, and ordinances which
are absolute, eternal, unchanging, taught by Apostles and
prophets, and clearly defined in the standard works of the
Church.

Still another approach Satan uses, especially perhaps
with the intellectually inclined, is to have us think "there
is no hell; and . . . I am no devil, for there is none" (2
Nephi 28:22). Without the devil there is no evil, except the
evil which individual societies condemn. Moral truth becomes relative, God is dethroned, and man is elevated to
become the measure of right and wrong. Satan again is
pleased, as philosophies multiply and the pride of men and
their wisdom carries them swiftly away from God.

Satan has a variety of "tools" at his disposal to use
against us, just as a fisherman has a variety of lures to at-
tract fish to take the bait.

An old legend tells of an Eskimo who was losing his
meat to a particularly crafty wolf. One day the Eskimo
took his razor-sharp knife and placed it blade up in the
snow. He then put a big piece of meat on top of the blade so
that all the wolf would see was the meat. The wolf came
and began enjoying the easy meal. The meat was so deli-
cious that he did not notice that as he was eating, he was
cutting his tongue on the knife. The wolf was literally
drinking his own blood, which went on until he became so
weak that he froze to death.

As in the story of the Eskimo, Satan tempts us with al-
luring distractions, attitudes, and circumstances which appear, on the surface, to be harmless; but as one partakes,
the spirit slowly suffers, creating a weakened condition
which can produce eventual alienation from God.

Jesus told his disciples in ancient America to "watch and pray always lest ye enter into temptation; for Satan desireth to have you, that he may sift you as wheat" (3 Nephi 18:18).

For What Things Should We Watch?

In these latter days there are many temptations and distractions which members of the Church must deal with in their quest to stay on course to eternal life. Apathy, discouragement, personal tragedy, intellectualism, boredom, interpersonal conflicts, divorce, materialism, immorality, and myriad related sins make up a partial list of things that can destroy faith. Discussed here are three prominent temptations which have claimed masses of individuals as victims, including whole nations.

1. *Pride—an enemy of Christ.* Pride is a foundation of sin and spawns a multitude of abominations. Pride is an enemy of Christ that was victorious over the entire Nephite civilization (see 1 Nephi 12:19). If one is climbing a ladder of sin, pride is a bottom rung. From there one ascends to greater heights of wickedness. As with the Nephites, pride can lead to swelling and boasting; then to envy and strife; then to malice and persecution; and finally, if unchecked, to the grievous sin of murder (see Helaman 13:22).

Pride separates people as they lift themselves away from their neighbors to a position of supposed superiority. Nephi said: "Because of pride, and wickedness, and abominations, and whoredoms, they have all gone astray save it be a few, who are the humble followers of Christ; nevertheless, they are led, that in many instances they do err because they are taught by the precepts of men" (2 Nephi 28:14). Could it be that those Nephi was referring to are, in part, members of The Church of Jesus Christ of Latter-day Saints who have erred because they have yielded to the persistent encroachment of the world? Because of pride, some members of the Church are tempted to seek praise and gain from Babylon, sometimes even at the expense of their commitment to Zion. President Joseph F. Smith foresaw three temptations that the Church would face in the twentieth century. He said: "There are at least three dangers that threaten the Church within, and the authorities need to awaken to the fact that the people should be warned unceasingly against them. As I see these, they are flattery of prominent men in the world, false educational ideas, and sexual impurity."[3]

2. *The quest for material riches.* In the Sermon on the Mount, Jesus told the Apostles to "seek . . . first the kingdom of God" (Matthew 6:33). He also said, "No man can serve two masters: for either he will hate the one, and love the other; or else he will hold to the one, and despise the other. Ye cannot serve God and mammon" (riches). (Matthew 6:24.) The acquisition of wealth often demands uncontested devotion. This devotion creates the danger of shifting what we "seek first." Priorities can become centered in those things which can be seen and owned instead of kingdoms and riches only visible with the eye of faith. People can forget God, or perhaps even unconsciously place his work further down on their list of priorities, as they run the race for more and more possessions.

In the Doctrine and Covenants we read: "And if ye seek the riches which it is the will of the Father to give unto you, ye shall be the richest of all people, for ye shall have the riches of eternity; and it must needs be that the riches of the earth are mine to give; but beware of pride, lest ye become as the Nephites of old" (D&C 38:39).

Consistently, the Nephites as a people became proud after they obtained prosperity. Pride separates people when some suppose themselves to be superior. When this happens it is impossible to keep the first and second commandments—to love God and to love our neighbor as ourselves. The broader application of this principle encompasses anything that creates unrighteous pride and thus separates people into "class distinctions."

Satan is pleased when he can get people overcommitted to things to the point that they distract them from building the kingdom of God. Whether the distraction is a material object, a profession, a hobby, or a business, if the gospel is squeezed out to the peripheral area of one's life Satan is achieving success.

3. *Immorality.* In a religious symposium at Brigham Young University, Clyde J. Williams spoke about the increasing plague of immorality:

> Immorality and all of its deviations is more and more becoming a destroyer of faith. One recent survey showed that 78 percent of Americans between the ages of 18–29 saw nothing wrong with a man and a woman having sexual relations before marriage. Video, cable, and satellite innovations have made sexually explicit material available in the privacy of our homes. Satan has thus found ways to pierce the armor of those who avoided immorality because of possible public exposure.[4]

Referring to this problem, Elder Vaughn J. Featherstone told the following story:

> I visited a stake in a distant city. I make it a custom to memorize their statistics, which at least gives me some slight understanding of activity levels. In this stake almost every statistic was down dramatically, including sacrament meeting, priesthood meeting, Relief Society, Primary, Sunday School, youth activity, tithing, and temple activity. I think I had a sense of righteous indignation, maybe even anger, that we had let Satan take over so much real estate.
>
> I questioned the stake leaders, and together we prayed and pondered for an answer. It came. This stronghold community of the Church had not especially been aware of the subtleties of Satan's strategy. Many in this farming community had purchased satellite receivers, video shops had opened, and naive parents were letting R- and X-rated movies into their homes through satellite channels,

and the youth and even some parents were renting them. Imagine violating the second most sacred place on the earth, the homes of righteous Latter-day Saints.[5]

It is essential that we do not get caught in a slow descent in which we become desensitized to the permissiveness which has pervaded our society. It is very easy to fall into the trap of justifying unwholesome entertainment. The percentage of unacceptable material is growing, and more than ever before Latter-day Saints are having to make decisions about what they will and will not allow themselves to see in movies or on television.

King Benjamin told his people: "But this much I can tell you, that if ye do not watch yourselves, and your thoughts, and your words, and your deeds, and observe the commandments of God, and continue in the faith of what ye have heard concerning the coming of our Lord, even unto the end of your lives, ye must perish. And now, O man, remember, and perish not." (Mosiah 4:30.)

Overcoming the Opposition

How can we successfully overcome the many and varied attacks which Satan will most certainly use against us as we strive to do what is right? Listed here are four principles of protection which are all interrelated.

1. *Build a foundation on Christ.* A physical foundation provides the supporting base which holds a structure together. Spiritual foundations, built by operating one's life according to true religious principles, give stability to life and strength to withstand opposition. The prophet Nephi, son of Helaman, taught:

> And now, my sons, remember, remember that it is upon the rock of our Redeemer, who is Christ, the Son of God, that ye must build your foundation; that when the devil shall send forth his mighty winds, yea, his shafts in the whirlwind, yea, when all his hail and his mighty storm

shall beat upon you, it shall have no power over you to drag you down to the gulf of misery and endless wo, because of the rock upon which ye are built, which is a sure foundation, a foundation whereon if men build they cannot fall (Helaman 5:12).

To build a foundation on Christ means to accept him as the true Messiah and make his atonement effective through obedience to the principles and ordinances of the gospel. When we build our lives around the doctrine of Christ, the "gates of hell shall not prevail against [us]."

In Lehi's dream the "great and spacious building" was unique in that it was lifted above the ground—it had no foundation. This building was a symbol of the pride and wisdom of the world. There is no stability or strength in trusting in the arm of flesh. When hearts are set upon the things of the world, people are "left unto themselves." The things cherished are of no worth and are subject to rust and corruption.

Shallow-rooted trees are soon destroyed during billowing storms. When we have a foundation built upon the Savior the promise is that the depth of our roots will be sufficient to withstand any storm or obstacle placed in our way. We can lay claim to the promise that the Lord is bound when we do what he says (see D&C 82:10).

2. *Live righteously*. Righteousness has always been the real armor of protection for God's people. Even when the odds have been in favor of the opposition, the Lord's people have prevailed as they relied first upon *his* arm and not the arm of flesh. Repeatedly the Nephites successfully repelled the attacking Lamanites because of their faith in Jesus Christ. Reporting on a vision of the latter days, Nephi wrote: "And it came to pass that I, Nephi, beheld the power of the Lamb of God, that it descended upon the saints of the church of the Lamb, and upon the covenant people of the Lord, who were scattered upon all the face of the earth; and they were armed with righteousness and with the power of God in great glory" (1 Nephi 14:14).

Commenting further, he wrote, "And the righteous need not fear, for they are those who shall not be confounded" (1 Nephi 22:22).

Adherence to true principles, or obedience to God's commandments, enlists the Lord in the protective service of the faithful. Anciently, the Lord pronounced a law whereby nations could be justified in entering armed conflict.

> And again, this is the law that I gave unto mine ancients, that they should not go out unto battle against any nation, kindred, tongue, or people, save I, the Lord, commanded them.
>
> And if any nation, tongue, or people should proclaim war against them, they should first lift a standard of peace unto that people, nation, or tongue;
>
> And if that people did not accept the offering of peace, neither the second nor the third time, they should bring these testimonies before the Lord;
>
> Then I, the Lord, would give unto them a commandment, and justify them in going out to battle against that nation, tongue, or people.
>
> And I, the Lord, would fight their battles, and their children's battles, and their children's children's, until they had avenged themselves on all their enemies, to the third and fourth generation. (D&C 98:33–37.)

In summary, if the first two requirements for justification are adhered to (the Lord commands, and an attempt at peace is first made), the promise is that the Lord will fight the battle for the righteous. The scriptures contain examples showing that the Lord directly intervenes to deliver the righteous. "The sun stood still" to help Joshua (see Joshua 10:12–13); a deep sleep came upon the Lamanites to aid the escape of Alma's people (see Mosiah 24:19); the Lord opened a sea for Moses and the children of Israel and then closed it upon the pursuing enemy (see Exodus 14).

In our personal struggle to endure in righteousness to the end of our lives, if we adhere to the standards of the Lord he will fight our battles for us. He will hedge up the way of our enemies, give us revelation, directly intervene, and deliver us from our enemies.

3. *Fortify weak areas.* In approximately 74 B.C. Captain Moroni met Zerahemnah on the banks of the river Sidon and a fierce battle ensued. There was a great difference in the preparation of the Nephite and the Lamanite soldiers.

> And when the armies of the Lamanites saw that the people of Nephi, or that Moroni, had prepared his people with breastplates and with arm-shields, yea, and also shields to defend their heads, and also they were dressed with thick clothing—
>
> Now the army of Zerahemnah was not prepared with any such thing; they had only their swords and their cimeters, their bows and their arrows, their stones and their slings; and they were naked, save it were a skin which was girded about their loins; yea, all were naked, save it were the Zoramites and the Amalekites.
>
> But they were not armed with breastplates, nor shields —therefore, they were exceedingly afraid of the armies of the Nephites because of their armor, notwithstanding their number being so much greater than the Nephites.
>
> And the work of death commenced on both sides, but it was more dreadful on the part of the Lamanites, for their nakedness was exposed to the heavy blows of the Nephites with their swords and their cimeters, which brought death almost at every stroke. (Alma 43:19–21; 37.)

Two years later, Amalickiah had gained control of the Lamanite kingdom and again waged war against the Nephites. This time they took great effort to prepare themselves with armor so that the Nephites would not have so great an advantage. Amalickiah's strategy was to attack the weaker cities first, so he marshaled his troops to the city of Ammonihah.

> And behold, the city had been rebuilt, and Moroni had stationed an army by the borders of the city, and they had cast up dirt round about to shield them from the arrows

and the stones of the Lamanites; for behold, they fought with stones and with arrows.

Behold, I said that the city of Ammonihah had been rebuilt. I say unto you, yea, that it was in part rebuilt, and because the Lamanites had destroyed it once because of the iniquity of the people, they supposed that it would again become an easy prey for them.

But behold, how great was their disappointment; for behold, the Nephites had dug up a ridge of earth round about them, which was so high that the Lamanites could not cast their stones and their arrows at them, that they might take effect, neither could they come upon them save it was by their place of entrance.

Now at this time the chief captains of the Lamanites were astonished exceedingly, because of the wisdom of the Nephites in preparing their place of security.

Now the leaders of the Lamanites had supposed, because of the greatness of their numbers, yea, they supposed that they should be privileged to come upon them as they had hitherto done; yea, and they had also prepared themselves with shields, and with breastplates; and they had also prepared themselves with garments of skins, yea, very thick garments to cover their nakedness.

And being thus prepared, they supposed that they should easily overpower and subject their brethren to the yoke of bondage, or slay and massacre them according to their pleasure.

But behold, to their uttermost astonishment, they were prepared for them, in a manner which never had been known among the children of Lehi. Now they were prepared for the Lamanites, to battle after the manner of the instructions of Moroni.

And it came to pass that the Lamanites, or the Amalickiahites, were exceedingly astonished at their manner of preparation for war. (Alma 49:2–7.)

The Lamanites withdrew their plans to attack Ammonihah and "retreated into the wilderness, and took their camp, and marched toward the land of Noah, supposing that to be the next best place for them to come against the Nephites" (Alma 49:12).

But behold, to their astonishment, the city of Noah, which had hitherto been a weak place, had now, by the means of Moroni, become strong, yea, even to exceed the strength of the city of Ammonihah.

And now, behold, this was the wisdom in Moroni; for he had supposed that they would be frightened at the city of Ammonihah; and as the city of Noah had hitherto been the weakest part of the land, therefore they would march thither to battle; and thus it was according to his desires. (Alma 49:14–15.)

Again Moroni prevailed in his righteous efforts to defeat the onslaught of Lamanite aggression. Perhaps one lesson that could be learned from the experiences of Captain Moroni, Zerahemnah, and Amalickiah, is the eventual triumph of the righteous. When Satan raised up an Amalickiah, the Lord raised up a Moroni. When Satan hedges up our way with temptations, the Lord will provide an avenue for our escape.

Satan is "careful" in his planning and strategic in his efforts. In his wisdom, he works on our weak areas, or worldly inclinations. President Harold B. Lee said:

Using words that are common to modern warfare, we might say that there are in the world today fifth columnists [spies] who are seeking to infiltrate the defense of every one of us, and when we lower those defenses, we open avenues to an invasion of our souls. There are carefully charted on the maps of the opposition the weak spots in every one of us. They are known to the forces of evil, and just the moment we lower the defense of any one of those ports, that becomes the D-Day of our invasion and our souls are in danger.[6]

In this regard, a wise plan on our part would be to take an inventory of our lives and seek to discover where our weaknesses really are. Then with a well-mapped plan of action, making workable goals as Captain Moroni did, we should fortify those areas against attack. Why leave an entrance open to an uninvited guest whose declared mission is to separate us eternally from God? Again, it is good for us to remember that one of the subtleties of Satan includes the teaching that there is no enemy to fortify against (see 2 Nephi 28:22).

4. *Control your circumstances.* In speaking on the subject of chastity, a wise stake president once told his audience that "chastity is not a matter of testimony and upbringing, but a matter of biology and circumstance."

How true that is! Good people fall, to their own surprise and the surprise of others, because a particular circumstance was too overpowering to resist. People initially sin in seclusion, either alone or with friends that consent. Have you ever known a priest who smoked his first cigarette at a Church function in front of his quorum? Can you recall any couples who lost their virtue while on a group date? Environment invites behavior.

As a bishop, I found there were three constants that almost always surfaced when I was interviewing ward members who had transgressed the law of chastity: *the two persons were alone; it was late at night; and they were in a secluded area.*

En route from California to Utah in a single engine airplane, I started to become nervous as we hit some turbulent air. My friend, who was the pilot, sensed my worry and asked me if I thought we were going to fall out of the sky. I mentioned that there seemed to be a lot of small airplane crashes and asked him if he ever worried about crashing. There is a wise message in his response to my question. He said that in the past he had made a study of aviation accident reports involving light aircraft. He had found that most accidents occurred at night or during bad weather. Then with a smile he said, "I don't fly at night, and I don't fly in bad weather." Many parallels to his response can be drawn.

Much heartache can be avoided, by so many, by applying this pilot's resolution. On dates young people may resolve: "I won't do this, and I won't do that. I won't be alone, behind closed doors, in seclusion, late at night, with someone of the opposite sex.'' If this resolve were made and implemented there would be no accidents and no surprises, because the circumstances which might give way to compromise would be recognized and avoided.

The key to increasing the likelihood of successfully enduring to the end is to recognize environments that encourage righteousness and then invite them into our lives. On the other hand, we must develop the ability to recognize situations (and people) that invite sin, and then avoid them.

5

The Power of Testimony

In the writings of John we read about Jesus miraculously feeding a multitude of five thousand people (see John 6). Those who had witnessed the miracle wanted Jesus to be their king. The Savior declined and departed into the mountains alone while the twelve Apostles set sail for Capernaum. A storm arose and the Master came to his disciples by walking on the water. The next day the people who had been with Jesus the day before went to Capernaum to find him.

> And when they had found him on the other side of the sea, they said unto him, Rabbi, when camest thou hither?
> Jesus answered them and said, Verily, verily, I say unto you, Ye seek me, not because ye saw the miracles, but because ye did eat of the loaves, and were filled. (John 6:25–26.)

Jesus' reply reflected his ability to discern the degree of spiritual understanding and commitment in others. The Savior knew the hearts of the people. He proceeded to teach them some deeply symbolic concepts about his earthly mission. He declared himself to be the "bread of Life," and said that man must eat of this bread to receive eternal life. When he had completed his message, the people said it was "a hard saying; who can hear it?" Then came a very sad moment: "From that time many of his disciples went back, and walked no more with him." (John 6:51, 54, 66.)

In this instance Jesus did not defer proclamation about the true nature of his mission, even though he knew it would offend *some* people. A physical foundation for testimony based on the multiplication of loaves and fishes was not adequate to sustain their discipleship. Jesus then turned to the twelve Apostles and said: "Will ye also go away?" Peter's reply marked the difference between himself and those who "walked no more" with Jesus. "Lord, to whom shall we go? thou hast the words of eternal life . . . we believe and are sure that thou art that Christ, the Son of the living God." (John 6:67–69.)

What was the source of Peter's testimony in comparison to the multitude who had witnessed the miracle yet had rejected the "hard" doctrine? The key is found in a conversation Jesus had at one point with the Twelve on the coasts of Caesarea Philippi.

> When Jesus came into the coasts of Caesarea Philippi, he asked his disciples, saying, Whom do men say that I the Son of man am?
>
> And they said, Some say that thou art John the Baptist: some, Elias; and others, Jeremias, or one of the prophets.
>
> He saith unto them, But whom say ye that I am?
>
> And Simon Peter answered and said, Thou art the Christ, the Son of the living God.
>
> And Jesus answered and said unto him, Blessed art thou, Simon Barjona: *for flesh and blood hath not revealed it unto thee, but my Father which is in heaven.* (Matthew 16:13–17; italics added.)

That is the sustaining key—a testimony that comes through revelation from God; a personal witness that is imprinted in the heart. If we know the basics, and those basics are grounded with spiritual confirmation from the Holy Ghost, when the "hard" doctrine comes or when Satan sends his "shafts in the whirlwind" (see Helaman 5:12) we will find in the depths of our souls the necessary strength to endure.

The Necessity of Personal Testimony

As John the Baptist was preaching at the river Jordan, the people "mused" in their hearts as to whether he was the Christ. He then distinguished his mission from the Savior's by telling of one mightier than himself who would come and baptize with the Holy Ghost. Of the Savior's mission John continued: "Whose fan is in his hand, and he will throughly purge his floor, and will gather the wheat into his garner; but the chaff he will burn with fire unquenchable" (Luke 3:17). What John seems to be saying here is that our discipleship will be tested. The wheat, represented by the faithful, will be separated from the chaff, or those who "walk no more with Jesus" after experiencing adversity. On the straight and narrow path we will meet tests and experiences that will have a separating effect.

In a BYU devotional address, President Harold B. Lee quoted a prophecy made by Heber C. Kimball:

"For, I say unto you, there is a test, there is a test, there is a test coming! and who will be able to stand. You imagine," said he, "that you would have stood by the Prophet Joseph, for many have said that they would like to have been associated with him. That you would have stood by him when persecution raged and he was assailed by foes within and without. You would have defended him and been true to him in the midst of every trial. You think you would have been delighted to have shown your integrity in the days of mobs and traitors. Let me say to you that many of you will see the time when you will have all the trouble and trial and persecution that you can stand and plenty of opportunities to show that you are true to God and His work.

"This church has before it many close places through which you will have to pass before the work of God is crowned with victory. To meet the difficulties that are coming, it will be necessary for you to have a knowledge of the truth of the work for yourselves. The difficulties will be of such a character that the man or woman who does not possess this personal knowledge or witness will fall. If you have not got that testimony, live right and call upon the Lord, and cease not until you obtain it. If you do not, you will not stand. Remember these things, for many of you will live to see them fulfilled. The time will come when no man, nor woman, will be able to endure on borrowed light. Each will have to be guided by the light within himself."

President Lee then made this commentary:

. . . This is the time of which President Kimball spoke, when he uttered that inspired declaration when each will have to stand on his own feet, and no man will be able to exist and stand on borrowed light. Each, for himself, must have an unshakable testimony of the divinity of this work, if he is to stand in this day.[1]

The Testimony We Need

What testimony do we need to sustain us to the end? Elder Bruce R. McConkie listed three vital elements of testimony: (1) to know that Jesus Christ is the divine son of God and the Savior of the world; (2) to know that Joseph Smith is the Prophet of God through whom the gospel was restored; and (3) to know that The Church of Jesus Christ of Latter-day Saints is the only true and living Church on the face of the earth.[2]

When we consider our testimonies we need to make certain that we are not solely basking in the fruits of Mormonism or, as the scripture says, "eating the bread and being filled." This could be defined as a personal commitment to the gospel that is based primarily on an attachment or attraction to the effective programs offered in the Church. We must have a deep care and abiding concern for the roots of Mormonism. One cannot truly enjoy the fruits of Mormonism without understanding the roots of Mormonism. These roots are modern revelation, priesthood, prophets, the divine calling of Joseph Smith, and the Book of Mormon. We need to attend and stay close to these roots.

Shortly after my baptism into the Church, I moved to a new location in Hawaii. In a conversation with my neighbor I mentioned that I had just been baptized into the LDS Church. She then told me that she had been a Mormon for twenty-five years but had joined another church during the past year. During our conversation she mentioned that she had enjoyed teaching Primary. For years she was a Primary worker, including being a member of the stake Primary presidency. I asked her if she had ever read the Book of Mormon. She had not. I asked her if she had ever prayed to know if the Church was true. Again, she had not. She said she "just enjoyed the Primary work." "What happened?" I inquired. Her simple reply was: "I got released." The light kindled through involvement in a Church program couldn't sustain her activity in the absence of the basic roots of testimony. For her, being released from a Church program meant being released from the Church.

There is a great difference in faith between those whose testimonies are grounded in the basic doctrines of the Church and those who are only socially impressed or whose activity is based upon a program or an individual. Every member of the Church should be able to answer yes to the following questions:

1. Have I read the root of Mormonism, the Book of Mormon, from cover to cover?

2. Have I prayed to gain a personal witness of its truthfulness?

3. Do I know by the power of the Holy Ghost that it is true?

President Ezra Taft Benson made the following comment concerning the importance of the Book of Mormon to members of the Church: "The Book of Mormon is the keystone of testimony. Just as the arch crumbles if the keystone is removed, so does all the Church stand or fall with the truthfulness of the Book of Mormon."[3]

In general conference, Elder Bruce R. McConkie delivered a sermon entitled "What Think Ye of the Book of Mormon?" At the conclusion of his remarks he issued a challenge: As we read each page of the Book of Mormon we should ask ourselves, "Could any man have written this book?" Elder McConkie then stated that, as we do this, we will come to know for ourselves that the book is true.[4]

The Blessings of Testimony

What a blessing it is to have a testimony—truth revealed anew. God does care, and he is doing something about it. Testimony provides the ingredient so vital to our progress. It gives us a purpose in life. It has been said that a man does not really begin to live until he knows what he is willing to die for. The individual who knows the why of his course of action is the one who can stick to his task. Others might lose their will to endure as stresses mount; the gospel becomes "inconvenient" as the demands of discipleship are increased.

It was faith born of testimony that helped sustain the sons of Mosiah as they labored among their brethren the Lamanites for fourteen years. The chains they were shackled with in the prison at Middoni didn't weaken their persistence or shorten their missions. The knowledge that a promised land lay ahead straightened Nephi's back, and fixed his determination through eight years of wilderness travel and numerous attempts on his life. Noah's faith sustained him during one hundred twenty years of rejection, after which only eight souls were saved in the ark. Stephen, being full of the Holy Ghost, and beholding God with Jesus on his right hand, peacefully met his death, forgiving those who ruthlessly took his life.

Testimony helps us to endure the suffering that is part of mortal life. It shapes our attitudes on how we view the events that happen around us. Consider the following statement by C. S. Lewis: "I believe in Christianity as I believe that the sun has risen, not only because I see it but because by it I see everything else."[5] When we view life through a gospel perspective we can see purpose in events that would otherwise crush and destroy us. We are sustained in our desire and ability to "fear not" and to "be of good cheer." Understanding the nature of our mortal probation, we comprehend design in suffering and heartache.

Through the eyes of testimony, death is seen as a necessary part to fulfill the *merciful plan* of the great Creator" (2 Nephi 9:6; italics added). Although death brings sorrow, relief comes with a bright hope in the resurrection. Knowledge of the purpose and design of mortality, which the Holy Ghost backs by a confirmation of its truthfulness, can most certainly smooth the rough waters we frequently pass through.

The following are excerpts from two letters that illustrate the perspective that testimony can produce in faithful individuals. A couple, who are friends of my family, gave birth to a son, Zachary. They wrote:

> Zachary was born with a major obstacle to overcome— S.E.D. Congenital Dwarfism. This is a rare form of dwarfism; the chance of being born with it is one in 50,000, we have been told. This is a genetic birth defect that has a

number of problems—the major one being a lack of normal growth in certain bones. His projected height will be somewhere between 29″ and 50″. His rib cage is too small for his lungs to fully expand, thus causing respiratory problems at birth that kept him in the hospital for two weeks until his body began to compensate. He has a cleft palate that affects only the soft palate, and will be easy to repair sometime in his second year. Zachary was also born with one club foot that is being corrected with a cast that is changed weekly at Johns Hopkins Hospital in Baltimore. Liz is really getting to know her way around that city! A double hernia, also part of S.E.D., was operated on successfully when Zachary was 6 weeks old. He will start wearing glasses this month as nearsightedness is another trait this dwarfism brings with it. Despite his small skinny body, Zachary is a cute and lovable baby with a sweet disposition. As he smiles and coos and looks up at us so very trusting and innocent, we feel our lives enriched and we think he will have a profound effect not only on us, but on others as well. He is a constant reminder to us of the values and priorities that bring true joy and happiness. As well, he is a graphic reminder that emphasis on looks is vanity at the least.

In January we received another letter. It was the program for Zachary's funeral. Part of the program was a letter to friends and family. It read:

Thursday morning when we arose and discovered Zachary had been called home, our tears flowed freely and we held his precious body near, feeling the tremendous love that had grown in our hearts for him. We knelt to thank our Heavenly Father for his time with us and felt so strongly of our Heavenly Father's spirit that the pain of death was not there—only a peace in the knowledge that our Father had indeed called his little one home to him.

The greatest joy this life has to offer is to love and to be loved. Zachary brought us much joy. He touched many lives in his short time on earth and helped us to know many of you we would not otherwise know. For this we are thankful. Zachary was able to help us discover the real essence of life. The body we come to earth to obtain is sacred, for it is the tabernacle of the spirit. But the outward appearance is really of no value. Without love it is a miserable existence. Zachary was well loved. The moment Dr. Lopits and his nurse, Diane Davis, saw him, we felt an outpouring of love from them. Many, many others gave likewise. We felt it. We know Zachary felt it.

Our hearts and minds are full this day. The glorious truths of the gospel of Jesus Christ let us know that Zachary still lives and that, in time, when Christ returns to this earth again, Zachary will come also with a strong, whole, perfect body for us to hold and raise from when he left us at 5 months old. . . .

We do not know why Zachary was called home on January 19, 1984. His Heavenly Father knows and that is sufficient for us. God lives. He is in control. This is His plan. The restored gospel teaches us the joy and gives us the strength of conviction to see us through the unknown with promptings and directions. God lives and blesses us. . . .

Zachary touched many lives. The purity and angelic qualities of this young son caused a stranger on an airplane to ask if he could hold him a little longer, just a few more moments.

We had the profound joy of holding Zachary for a few moments.

What a marvelous perspective and glorious hope a testimony of the gospel of Jesus Christ instills in the hearts of those who have paid the price to receive it, and who are faithfully cultivating its increase!

In his elegant manner, President Kimball enumerated the blessings of testimony:

A sure knowledge of the spiritual is an open door to rewards attainable and joys unspeakable. To ignore the testimony is to grope in caves of impenetrable darkness; to creep along in fog over hazardous highways. That person is to be pitied who may still be walking in darkness at noonday, who is tripping over obstacles which can be removed, and who dwells in the dim flickering candlelight of insecurity and skepticism. The testimony is the electric light illuminating the cavern; the wind and sun dissipating the fog; the power equipment removing boulders from the road. It is the mansion on the hill replacing the shack in the marshes; the harvester shelving the sickle and cradle; the tractor, train, automobile, and plane displacing the ox team. It is the rich, nourishing kernels of corn instead of the husks in the trough. It is much more than all else, for "this is life eternal, that they might know thee the only true God, and Jesus Christ, whom thou hast sent." (John 17:3.)[6]

Testimony and Persecution

In the Church, we are bold when bearing testimony. "God lives," we say; "Jesus is divine!"; "Joseph Smith saw God the Father and Jesus Christ!"; "There was an apostasy necessitating restoration!"; "Of the multitude of churches, there is one church, and only one church, that is authorized, commissioned, and true."

These are bold statements. Peter and John were not afraid to state them in their ministries. Stephen didn't hesitate to declare them before those who would shortly thereafter take his life. Paul certainly wasn't afraid to say them, and neither was Joseph Smith. Said Joseph about his experience in the grove: "I had actually seen a light, and in the midst of that light I saw two Personages, and they did in reality speak to me; . . . For I had seen a vision; I knew it, and I knew that God knew it, and I could not deny it, neither dared I do it; at least I knew that by so doing I would offend God, and come under condemnation" (Joseph Smith—History 1:25).

The Church has been persecuted since its beginning. Persecution can strengthen our testimonies—if the stories of Palmyra and Cumorah were false, Satan would not have raised his hand against them.

In a general conference address, President Gordon B. Hinckley said: "We now seem to have a great host of critics. Some appear intent on trying to destroy us. They belittle that which we call divine. In their cultivated faultfinding, they see not the majesty of the great onrolling of this cause."[7]

In a local newspaper in Provo, Utah, there had been an ongoing series of articles written by individuals who wanted to persuade LDS Church members to leave the Church. In response to the highly critical and spirited remarks, a local member wrote this rebuttal:

> Editor:
> I have been thinking of quitting the Mormon Church. Yes, if I can, I am going to get even with that church. As soon as I can find another church that teaches about the Gathering of the House of Israel; the return of the Ten Tribes and their mission; the return of the Jews to Palestine and why, and how, they are going to build the temple; the building of temples and what to do in them; the mission of Elias, the prophet, as predicted by Malachi; the method for the salvation of the people that died at the time of Noah, in the flood; the origin of the American Indian; the complete explanation of why Jesus of Nazareth had to have a mortal mother but not a mortal father; the explanation of the three degrees of glory (three heavens) as mentioned by Paul; the complete explanation of why Elias and Moses did not die but had to be translated (since they both lived before the resurrection was introduced by Christ); the restoration of the gospel by modern revelation as promised by Peter and Paul and Jesus himself; the belief in eternal marriage and the family, and the knowledge and the place to seal for eternity; that teaches abstinence from all harmful drugs and foods; and that sells the best fire insurance policy on earth, for the last days, for only a 10th of my income.
>
> Yes, sir, as soon as I can find another church that teaches all that, or even half as much, I will say good-bye to this Mormon Church. The church that I am looking for must also be able to motivate 30,000 youth, and adults,

for the second or third time, to leave their homes for two years at their own expense and go to far-away places to teach and preach without salary. It must be able to call, on a frosty day, some 5 or 6 thousand professors, students, lawyers, doctors, judges, policemen, businessmen, housewives, children, and even the pets of the family, to go and pick apples at 6 a.m. It must be able to call meetings and get the attention for two hours of more than 150,000 men. Yes, it must also teach and show why salvation is assured for children who die before eight years of age.

Mr. Editor, could you help me find a church that teaches all that and more than a hundred other doctrines and principles, which I have no room to mention here, and which brings solace, comfort to the soul, peace, hope, and salvation to mankind, and above all, that answers the key questions that all the great philosophers have asked; questions and answers that explain the meaning of life, the purpose of death, suffering and pain; the absolute need for a Redeemer and the marvelous plan conceived and executed by Jesus Christ the Savior? Yes, as soon as I find another church that teaches that and also that has the organization and the powers to make that teaching effective, I am going to quit the Mormon Church. For I should not tolerate that "they" should change a few words in the Book of Mormon—even if those changes simply improve the grammar and the syntax of the verses—for, after all, don't you think the Divine Church should employ angels as bookmakers, and clerks, to do all the chores on earth? Don't you think, Mr. Editor, that the Divine Church should also have prophets that don't get sick and don't get old and die, and certainly, that don't make a goof here and there. No, sir. A Divine Church should be so divine that only perfect people should belong to it, and only perfect people should run it. As a matter of fact, the Church should be so perfect that it should not even be here on earth!!!

So, I repeat, if any one of the kind readers of this imperfect letter knows about another church that teaches and does as much for mankind as the Mormon Church, please let me know. And please do it soon, because my turn to go to the cannery is coming up. Also, "they" want my last son—the fifth one—to go away for two years and again, I have to pay for all that. And I also know that they expect me to go to the farm to prune trees, and I have heard that our ward is going to be divided again, and it is our side that must build the new chapel. And also, someone the other day had the gall of suggesting that my wife and I get ready to go on a second mission, and when you come back, they said, you can volunteer as a temple worker. Boy, these Mormons don't leave you alone for a minute. And what do I get for all that, I asked? "Well," they said, "for one, you can look forward to a funeral service at no charge!" . . . Do you think you can help me to find another church?[8]

We have so much to be thankful for and we have so much to have a testimony of. The restoration of the gospel is truly a marvelous work and a wonder. When persecution comes our way, a testimony enables us to say, as did Peter: "Lord, to whom shall we go? thou hast the words of eternal life." (John 6:68.)

6

The Sustaining Vision

It is essential during our journey on the straight and narrow path to keep our mind's eye focused on eternal life. It is when we take our eye off our eternal goals that we risk costly delays and disastrous detours. Dreams vitalize and energize the human spirit. Each day we ought to hang a picture of celestial achievement before our waking eyes. People that achieve great things, dream great things. To dream is to see, taste, feel, and focus on a goal. A baseball player dreams of the World Series and focuses on each game and each time at bat. He realizes that to take his eye off the ball means a missed opportunity to take a good swing. A quarterback keeps his eye on the goal line and intensely plans and executes a strategy to progress, yard by yard, towards it. The mountain climber visualizes himself resting on the summit, and is careful to secure his every step. Similarly, pursuit of the celestial kingdom requires fidelity of purpose, a concerted effort, and adherence to the gospel plan.

Don't Settle for Less

It has been said that it is not self-discipline people lack in achieving their goals, but vision. Many people begin a program with full intention of reaching their goals but get distracted with peripheral issues. The original goal, dream, or priority then becomes buried beneath excuses, or lost, as impatience and expediency create contentment and a settling for less. If we could truly comprehend the riches of celestial inheritance, the blessings of Abraham, Isaac and Jacob, the minuteness of our mortal stay in comparison to eternity, and what it means to become a joint heir with Jesus Christ, no sacrifice would be too great, nor would the amount of patience and long-suffering required be too difficult to endure. Where there is no vision, achievement is stymied and dreams are lost.

Consider the End of Your Salvation

The scriptures speak of "considering the end of [our] salvation" (D&C 46:7). Alma, in trying to motivate the people of Zarahemla to repent, sought to get his listeners to visualize the judgment day and the alternatives of being found either worthy or unclean.

> Do ye exercise faith in the redemption of him who created you? *Do you look forward with an eye of faith,* and *view* this mortal body raised in immortality, and this corruption raised in incorruption, to stand before God to be judged according to the deeds which have been done in the mortal body?
>
> I say unto you, can you *imagine* to yourselves that ye hear the voice of the Lord, saying unto you, in that day: Come unto me ye blessed, for behold, your works have been the works of righteousness upon the face of the earth?
>
> Or do ye *imagine* to yourselves that ye can lie unto the Lord in that day, and say—Lord, our works have been righteous works upon the face of the earth—and that he will save you?

Or otherwise, can ye *imagine* yourselves brought before the tribunal of God with your souls filled with guilt
and remorse, having a remembrance of all your guilt, yea,
a perfect remembrance of all your wickedness, yea, a remembrance that ye have set at defiance the commandments of God?

I say unto you, can ye *look up to God* at that day with
a pure heart and clean hands? I say unto you, can you
look up, having the image of God engraven upon your
countenances? (Alma 5:15–19; italics added.)

Here, Alma does a masterful job in trying to shock his
people out of their sinful state by having them visualize the
reality of a future judgment. It is essential for us to comprehend that there *is* a relationship between what we do
here on earth and the reward we receive in the eternities.
The idea is that if we look forward, view, imagine and consider frequently our desired destination, our chances of
not getting lost during the journey due to shortsightedness
are increased.

Sustain the Journey with Vision

Keeping the end in mind helps to sustain us in our
quest for eternal life. One summer I went with my Utah
ward on the annual youth conference excursion. We
walked from Nephi to Manti. The first day we walked six-
teen miles, and the second day fourteen. On the second
day I served on the survival truck, administering water-
melon to the tired travelers. One of our youth was particularly tired. She had her head down and her limping revealed she had developed some severe blisters on her feet.
In a very touching scene, one member of the Young
Women presidency recognized the need to give this girl encouragement. She walked over, put her arm on the girl's
shoulder, and said—"Look!" The advisor then pointed to
the beautiful Manti Temple, which could now be seen. The
sight and beauty of the destination had a visible effect on
the young girl. She lifted her head, smiled, picked up her

pace, and kept moving forward. Likewise in life, the gentle
stirrings of the Spirit within is like an angel's touch, beckoning for us to "look" and behold the glories that await
those who keep moving forward on the straight and narrow
path.

Nephi had an entirely different perspective of his family's journey into the wilderness than did Laman and
Lemuel. Nephi said: "And so great were the blessings of
the Lord upon us, that while we did live upon raw meat in
the wilderness, our women did give plenty of suck for their
children, and were strong, yea, even like unto the men;
and they began to bear their journeyings without mur-
murings" (1 Nephi 17:2).

Nephi was able to press forward without murmuring
because he knew that there was a promised land ahead.
He had seen it in a vision, and this knowledge sustained
his enthusiasm to push forward.

Now compare Nephi's perception of the wilderness experience with Laman and Lemuel's:

> And thou art like unto our father, led away by the
> foolish imaginations of his heart; yea, he hath led us out
> of the land of Jerusalem, and we have wandered in the
> wilderness for these many years; and our women have
> toiled, being big with child; and they have borne children
> in the wilderness and suffered all things, save it were
> death; and it would have been better that they had died
> before they came out of Jerusalem than to have suffered
> these afflictions. Behold, these many years we have suf-
> fered in the wilderness, which time we might have en-
> joyed our possessions and the land of our inheritance;
> yea, and we might have been happy. (1 Nephi 17:20–21.)

Devoid of desire, righteous living, and the faith so evident in Nephi's life, for Laman and Lemuel there was no
eye of faith fixed on the promised land; there was no sustaining spiritual influence from the Holy Ghost; there was
no view of the eternal purposes of God, which view makes

momentary struggles seem insignificant. Laman and Lemuel were thus left to themselves to dwell on their afflictions and look backward at a land soon to be destroyed, and at possessions upon which their happiness depended.

A Church member who was struggling to complete his dissertation for his doctorate degree tells the following story, illustrating the sustaining power of keeping close to one's mind and heart a vision of the end of one's goal:

> I had just finished my master's degree. I had thought about getting a doctoral degree, but I was surprised when, after praying about it, I found myself impressed to start the following summer. In that prayer, in my mind's eye, the Lord let me see a vision of my graduation, and I knew it was a summer graduation ceremony.
>
> I went to school for four summers, one year and a spring. The last summer was spent completing my dissertation. I worked 10 to 14 hours everyday except Sunday. I had set a schedule for myself so that I could meet the deadline requirement for summer commencement, but I had fallen behind and I had become physically and mentally exhausted. One evening, at 10:30 p.m., I was studying and the library closed. I needed at least two or three more hours of study time to stay on schedule. I went out and got into my Volkswagon and lay down in the seat, feeling very discouraged, and ready to give up. I started entertaining plans to let summer graduation pass and to put my name on December's list. At that moment across my mind came again the impression of a summer graduation, and I was there. Because of that experience, I was able to pick myself up, go back into the computer room, stay on schedule, and graduate that August.[1]

"Die Well"

In the October 1976 general conference, Elder Sterling W. Sill gave a talk entitled, "To Die Well." He spoke of beginning with the end in mind:

And it has been said that the most important event in life is death. We live to die and then we die to live. Death is a kind of graduation day for life. It is our only means of entrance to our eternal lives. And it seems to me to be a very helpful procedure to spend a little time preliving our death. That is, what kind of person would you like to be when the last hour of your life arrives?

The last hour is the key hour. That is the hour that judges all of the other hours. No one can tell whether or not his life has been successful until his last hour.

Elder Sill then told the legend of Dr. John Faustus. Twenty-four years before his death, Faustus sold his soul to Satan. He told Satan "If you will aid me for twenty-four years, punishing my enemies and helping my friends, at the end of that time I will deliver up my soul." Elder Sill continued:

And then the twenty-four years began, and Faust had every experience of good and bad. But almost before he was aware, it was said to Faust as it must be said to every one of us, "Thine hour is come." Now, this is the first time that he had ever thought about the consequences of what he was doing. Only now did he discover how badly he had cheated himself. Then he wanted to revoke the bargain, but that was impossible. And then he prayed and he said, "Oh God, if thou canst have no mercy on my soul, at least grant some end to my incessant pain. Let Faustus live in hell a thousand years or even an hundred thousand, but at last be saved!"

But he knew that, according to his own bargain, even this could never be. And then during his last hour he sat and watched the clock tick off the seconds and finally, just as the hour struck, the last words of Faust before he died were: "Faustus is gone to hell!"

Now if Faust had lived his last hour first, he never would have permitted himself to come to this unprofitable place. I have a relative who, when she reads a novel, always reads the last chapter first. She wants to know before she begins where she is going to be when she gets through. And that is a pretty good idea for life.[2]

In contrast to the story Elder Sill related concerning the eternal torment of John Faustus, Elder Melvin J. Ballard published a story about a dream he had and the feelings it produced when he woke:

> When I was doing missionary work with some of our brethren, laboring among the Indians, seeking the Lord for light to decide certain matters pertaining to our work there, and receiving a witness from Him that we were doing things according to his will, I found myself one evening in the dreams of the night, in that sacred building, the Temple. After a season of prayer and rejoicing, I was informed that I should have the privilege of entering into one of those rooms to meet a glorious Personage, and as I entered the door, I saw, seated on a raised platform, the most glorious Being my eyes ever have beheld, or that I ever conceived existed in all the eternal worlds. As I approached to be introduced, He arose and stepped towards me with extended arms, and He smiled as He softly spoke my name. If I shall live to be a million years old, I shall never forget that smile. He took me into His arms and kissed me, pressed me to His bosom, and blessed me, until the marrow of my bones seemed to melt! When He had finished, I fell at His feet, and as I bathed them with my tears and kissed them, I saw the prints of the nails in the feet of the Redeemer of the world. The feeling that I had in the presence of Him who hath all things in His hands, to have His love, His affection, and His blessings are such that if I ever can receive that of which I had but a foretaste, I would give all that I am, all that I ever hope to be, to feel what I then felt.[3]

To endure to that glorious end would indeed be worth all that is in our power to do and to give. The wonderful part is that eternal life is within the grasp of all of us. It is very obtainable; the instructions are clear, and the manual is complete. There is room enough for all who will choose, by their own free will, to receive the inheritance a loving Father extends to his loved sons and daughters.

7

The Holy Ghost

After we are baptized we receive the gift of the Holy Ghost. This gift gives us the privilege of having the power and influence of the third member of the Godhead in our lives. The constancy of his effect upon us is dependent upon our continued worthiness.

The Holy Ghost has been assigned various roles as part of his stewardship. Each role or responsibility is specifically designed to help "bring to pass the immortality and eternal life of man" (Moses 1:39). His mission is to be of service to us—he ministers to us through his various roles, as the situation and circumstance requires.

Five Functions

Following are five functions of the Holy Ghost, each of which has a profound effect upon our ability to maintain our discipleship throughout this life's probationary state.

1. *A Constant Companion* (see D&C 121:46). We all have an inherent need for companionship. The gift of the

Holy Ghost, bestowed on us after baptism, provides us with a lifelong friend and traveling companion. Situations may arise that necessitate our being alone for a period of time—death of a spouse is an example. We do not, however, need to suffer loneliness. Relationships, as well as family ties, can indeed be renewed as righteous families, sealed in the temple, have the blessing of being together forever. In the meantime, the periods of seeming isolation can be lessened by one whose commission is to stay with, watch over, and lift those who remain qualified to have his influence.

2. *The Comforter* (see John 14:26). We live in a time of great stress. Prophecies depict our day as one in which "men's hearts shall fail them" (D&C 45:26). Divorce, delinquency, violence, terrorism, war, immorality, and general decadence are increasing in epidemic proportions. We worry about economic conditions, employment, sickness, and how to keep the persistent influences of an impure world out of the family circle.

The deep and abiding peace which surpasses condition and circumstance comes to us through Jesus Christ and is administered through the Holy Ghost. The "peace of God" comes into our lives as a result of our "faith and good works" (Alma 7:27). It enables us to see beyond the troubled moment and to gain solace through an eternal perspective. The warmth in the bosom is the whisper to the soul, "all is well, all is well." We might not immediately see how our problems will be resolved, but when light enters the depressed or discouraged chamber, windows are opened and new insights and solutions can now enter in.

Worry, loneliness, fear, confusion, grief, discouragement, and depression are all conditions understood by the Lord. Have you ever wondered how Jesus, the Good Shepherd, knows how to tend his sheep so well? Concerning Jesus' earthly ministry, Alma said to the people of Gideon:

And he shall go forth, suffering pains and afflictions
and temptations of every kind; and this that the word
might be fulfilled which saith he will take upon him the
pains and the sicknesses of his people.

And he will take upon him death, that he may loose
the bands of death which bind his people; and he will
take upon him their infirmities, that his bowels may be
filled with mercy, according to the flesh, that he may
know according to the flesh how to succor his people according to their infirmities. (Alma 7:11–12.)

Jesus knows our suffering, having experienced pains
"even more than man can suffer" (Mosiah 3:7); thus with
perfect empathy he can send the Comforter to administer
to us according to our various needs.

3. *The Testator* (see 3 Nephi 11:35–36). As the Testator, the Holy Ghost bears witness with an indelible assurance that the gospel path is true, and that at the end of the
prescribed course lies a most glorious reward. When dis-
couragements come and temptation advertises an alternative route, the impression of surety cancels our desire to
take a wrong turn and buoys us up to continue our charted
course.

Confidence comes through knowledge; courage
through assurance; and determination through testimony.
Endurance is sustained by the truth. The unique witness
which the Spirit administers to our hearts makes these
qualities available to us as we walk by faith throughout our
lives.

4. *The Sanctifier* (see 3 Nephi 27:20). What greater encouragement could there be than knowing that you are acceptable to God! The kingdom of heaven is not filthy, and
no unclean thing can enter therein (see 1 Nephi 15:34).
The atonement of Jesus Christ is the source of cleansing,
and the Holy Ghost is the agent that fulfills it. As we sincerely partake of the sacrament and repent of our mistakes, the warmth of the Spirit is the confirmation that we

have been forgiven, and that taste of heaven encourages us to conquer temptation for another week and press on in our purpose.

A member of the Church shared with me the following story in relation to the encouragement he felt when he knew he had received forgiveness. "I had struggled for a long time with whether or not I had been forgiven in my life of some particular sins of which I was really ashamed. One day I was walking across the campus at the Brigham Young University thinking about my life and the blessings which the Lord had given me. As my thinking continued in this direction, a sweeping feeling of warmth came over me. Into my mind came the knowledge that I had been forgiven. I was clean, and although past sins were history I need not be afflicted anymore by that history. At that time I truly knew what it meant to be born again. As Alma told Helaman, my joy was as exceeding as had been my pain (see Alma 36:20). This cleanliness produced hope, destroyed discouragement, and kindled a desire to move ahead in my life."

5. *A Revelator* (see D&C 8:2–3). The role of the Holy Ghost as a guide is of great significance in our lives. A mountain climbing guide knows the terrain. Having been on the mountain before, he knows the potential dangers. His sole purpose is to insure, as much as possible, a safe climb. He cannot take the steps for those he guides, but he does inform, caution, remind, instruct, and assist them. Similarly, the Holy Ghost is a guide, and learning to listen to his informed counsel can have a tremendous impact on our spiritual progress.

A Personal Liahona

Alma related to his son Helaman a story Helaman was probably already familiar with. Alma used this story to make a most important analogy.

And now, my son, I have somewhat to say concerning the thing which our fathers call a ball, or director—or our fathers called it Liahona, which is, being interpreted, a compass; and the Lord prepared it.

And behold, there cannot any man work after the manner of so curious a workmanship. And behold, it was prepared to show unto our fathers the course which they should travel in the wilderness.

And it did work for them according to their faith in God; therefore, if they had faith to believe that God could cause that those spindles should point the way they should go, behold, it was done; therefore they had this miracle, and also many other miracles wrought by the power of God, day by day.

Nevertheless, because those miracles were worked by small means it did show unto them marvelous works. They were slothful, and forgot to exercise their faith and diligence and then those marvelous works ceased, and they did not progress in their journey;

Therefore, they tarried in the wilderness, or did not travel a direct course, and were afflicted with hunger and thirst, because of their transgressions.

And now, my son, I would that ye should understand that these things are not without a shadow; for as our fathers were slothful to give heed to this compass (now these things were temporal) they did not prosper; even so it is with things which are spiritual.

For behold, it is as easy to give heed to the word of Christ, which will point to you a straight course to eternal bliss, as it was for our fathers to give heed to this compass, which would point unto them a straight course to the promised land.

And now I say, is there not a type in this thing? For just as surely as this director did bring our fathers, by following its course, to the promised land, shall the words of Christ, if we follow their course, carry us beyond this vale of sorrow into a far better land of promise. (Alma 37:38–45.)

What is the type and shadow Alma referred to? The symbolism is simple yet profound: Mortality is our wilderness; the far greater land of promise is the celestial kingdom; and our personal Liahona is the words of Christ.

If we exercise faith and diligence we will travel in a straight course, we will not tarry, or waste the days of our probation, and we can avoid many afflictions.

Nephi taught that the words of Christ are given to us by the Holy Ghost (see 2 Nephi 32:3, 5). If we have been baptized and confirmed we each have a personal Liahona which, through our faith and diligence, can point us in a direct course to eternal life. President Spencer W. Kimball compared our conscience to the Liahona:

> You must realize that you have something like the compass, like the Liahona, in your own system. Every child is given it. When he is eight years of age, he knows good from evil, if his parents have been teaching him well. If he ignores the Liahona that he has in his own makeup, he eventually may not have it whispering to him. But if we will remember that every one of us has the thing that will direct him aright, our ship will not get on the wrong course and suffering will not happen and bows will not break and families will not cry for food—if we listen to the dictates of our own Liahona, which we call the conscience.[1]

How Does Our Liahona Work?

Three consistent ingredients are evident as we analyze how the Holy Ghost functions as a guide in our lives.

1. In Moroni 7:13 we learn that everything that inviteth and enticeth to do good is inspired of God. So first we are invited by the Spirit to act. We, as Latter-day Saints, use many words or phrases to describe this invitation by the Spirit—"I feel prompted;" "I feel impressed;" "I feel assured;" "I feel warm;" "I feel peaceful;" "I am confident;" "It is clear;" "I feel calm;" "I feel a burning." Sometimes we talk about hearing a "still small voice." All of these terms are associated with knowing we are acting

righteously, or that the spindles are pointing in the right direction and we are following them.

2. After we have received the inspiration, faith and trust are expressed through actions, or by following the prompting. Lehi did not see the promised land from the wilderness, but he trusted Heavenly Father by following the pointers of the Liahona.

3. One receives a witness after the trial of one's faith (see Ether 12:6; John 7:17).

Concisely stated, a person feels the inspiration, then shows his faith by acting or by following the inspiration, after which comes the witness at an appropriate time in the wisdom of God.

Examples

There are many examples in the scriptures that illustrate these points. Through prayer, Nephi learned of the truth of his father's words (see 1 Nephi 2:16). When Lehi told his family about the Lord's desire for them to retrieve the brass plates from Laban, Nephi devotedly said that he would "go and do the things which the Lord hath commanded, for [he] knew that the Lord giveth no commandments unto the children of men, save he shall prepare a way for them that they may accomplish the thing which he commandeth them" (1 Nephi 3:7).

Nephi demonstrated his verbal expression of faith with action: "And I was led by the Spirit, not knowing beforehand the things which I should do" (1 Nephi 4:6). His witness came en route to Laban's treasury: "Nevertheless I went forth, and as I came near unto the house of Laban I beheld a man, and he had fallen to the earth before me, for he was drunken with wine" (1 Nephi 4:7).

Of this event, President Spencer W. Kimball said, "Remember again that no gates were open; Laban was not drunk; and no earthly hope was justified at the moment

Nephi exercised his faith and set out finally to get the plates."[2]

A good example of exercising one's faith comes from a book entitled *Others*, by Blaine and Brenton Yorgason:

> A woman, whose husband was away from home on business, was awakened one night feeling that she should get her little children outside and call the fire department. She led her children outside, wrapped them with blankets, and then went back in and phoned the fire department and reported a fire, though there was no sign of one in her home. Two or three minutes later, just as the fire truck was coming around the corner, there was an explosion and her home was engulfed in flames. She, too, had been willing and able to listen to the feelings of the Spirit.[3]

Looking back, we can find key words: "She *felt* she should get her children outside (the inspiration); she *led* her children outside (the faith); there *was* an explosion (the witness).

When President David O. McKay was a member of the Quorum of the Twelve Apostles, he visited Hawaii. There he went on an excursion to a volcano with a group of missionaries, where they stood on the rim of that fiery pit. Tiring of the cold, one of the group suggested that they move to a balcony a few feet down inside the crater, which had a protective railing. After they had been on the balcony for some little while, President McKay said, "Brethren, I feel impressed that we should get out of here." They climbed out, and almost immediately the entire balcony collapsed and fell into the molten lava below.[4]

Proselyting by the Spirit

As missionaries, we used our personal Liahonas. We called it, "proselyting by the Spirit." We would take our area and divide it up into sections, giving each section a number. As companions, we would take turns deciding

where to tract. The process required studying out each
section and then praying for a feeling of direction, or for
the "spindle" to point to a specific area. After obtaining a
good feeling for a particular area, we would then pour over
the streets within that area. What a marvelous experience
it was to feel the "spindles" turning to the streets of people
who were ready to hear the gospel of Jesus Christ! Sometimes answers came quickly, while other times we would
search and plead for much longer periods of time. One
time I emerged from the privacy of my morning prayers
and told my companion that I knew where we should pros-
elyte that day. The area and the street had come to me
quickly and clearly as I prayed for direction. With excite-
ment I said, "Let's go, Elder!"

We arrived at the street where I had felt we should tract
and to our great surprise it was a vacant lot! My companion must have wondered about my inspiration—not a door
in sight to knock on. I still felt the "spindles" turning,
however. I looked over and saw a car parked next to the
curb of the vacant area. I said to my companion, "This
must be it." We knocked on the car window and a man inside opened the door. We introduced ourselves and he invited us to get in. We taught him the first discussion in his
car. After we ended, he invited us to have some hot choc-
olate with him at a nearby hotel.

In our conversation at the hotel he asked us a question:
"Do you believe in divine providence?" I didn't know
what providence meant, so I asked him to explain. He then
told us that he felt he had parked next to the vacant lot for
the particular purpose of meeting us. "I had just been
driving around and felt that I should stop and sit," he said.
He then asked us if we agreed—that was the witness after
the faith.

Messages on Our Liahonas

In addition to pointing in the direction Lehi's family
should travel, the Liahona also provided written messages.

And it came to pass that I, Nephi, beheld the pointers which were in the ball, that they did work according to the faith and diligence and heed which we did give unto them.

And there was also written upon them a new writing, which was plain to be read, which did give us understanding concerning the ways of the Lord; and it was written and changed from time to time, according to the faith and diligence which we gave unto it. And thus we see that by small means the Lord can bring about great things. (1 Nephi 16:28–29.)

Messages change as the need arises and as the opposition changes. Like a coach, the Lord sends in new plays to counteract the opposing team.

A friend of mine was on a business trip in San Francisco. Having some spare time, he decided to see a movie. In the newspaper he saw a show advertised that he had heard friends speak of. The movie carried an X-rating but was said to have some redeeming qualities. He arrived at the theater and looked at the billboard; sure enough, there was the title and the X-rating. My friend progressed in line to buy tickets until he was eighth from the front. He reached for his wallet to get out the money, looking up again at the billboard. This time, however, there was a new title or "message." It read, "Do not buy into forbidden paths." The wallet was put back in place and my friend quickly left. The words, "Do not buy into forbidden paths," were a direct quote from his patriarchal blessing. In this instance the Holy Ghost retrieved the words of Christ, given by a patriarch, to point my friend away from an influence that could only be destructive.

Perhaps the most significant benefit from our personal Liahona is not the dramatic experiences, but the little nudges it gives us to be more patient; the gentle reminder that we forgot to apologize to our spouse; the invitation to spend more time with our children.

As we bump against the sides of the straight and narrow path which Jesus has set for us to walk on, we sometimes feel the withdrawal of the Spirit. This withdrawal is the signal for us to redirect our thinking or behavior. The Holy Ghost gives us the knowledge of whether we are going in the right direction in our quest for eternal life.

Elder F. Burton Howard made this remark at a BYU fireside:

> If we have been worthy, and if we have followed the guidance of the Spirit as manifested in the feelings of our hearts, then we can know beyond doubt that what is done was best. We can be certain, although there may have been trials, or we may be having difficulties, that we are where the Lord would have us be. We will know that, although the grass may seem greener elsewhere, our decision to enter the pasture we are in was prompted and purposeful and preparatory.[5]

A Friend and a Guide

Consider the following parable about the role of the Holy Ghost as a friend and a guide:

You are the son or daughter of a wealthy father. He has bequeathed to you, as his lawful heir, a vast fortune. This fortune was deposited in a far-off country and a map was given to you with exact details outlining your journey. A brother who lost his own inheritance knows of the journey you will make and, having nothing to lose himself, desires to kill you. He has posted his cohorts on the roads to the airports and has cunningly sought to cut off every possible route.

Perplexed and deeply concerned about your safety, but determined to possess your inheritance, you plan your departure.

Knowing the specific dangers of the road, your father sends a friend to your house with instructions to help you make a safe trip. The journey commences and although the enemy could be sighted to the left, to the right, and up ahead, your guide is ever present and his directions are clear. Following them brings peace, miraculous safety, and a most enjoyable tour of the country.[6]

Spiritually speaking, the father is Heavenly Father. The far-off country is heaven. The journey is the straight and narrow path, and the inheritance is eternal life. The brother and his cohorts are Satan and his angels. The friend sent to accompany you is the Holy Ghost.

We ought to pray for the sensitivity to feel the Spirit work in our lives, and then pray for the courage to follow it. What, then, do we do with all the witnesses that come after we exercise our faith? Perhaps we ought to save them in a "faith pile"—a compilation of our own faith-promoting experiences. If we are ever asked to climb Mount Moriah, as Abraham was when he was told to sacrifice Isaac, we will have the foundation to do as Abraham did—follow the Lord.

8

Safeguards Called Commandments

An understanding of the kindness and wisdom behind each of the commandments will increase our appreciation for them. This, in turn, can motivate obedience for a long period of time. One does not have to go far to hear statements like the following:

(A member of the Church to a friend who is a baptismal candidate): "Do you really know what you're getting into?"

(A student to a friend): "I'm not sure my wife and I knew what we were doing when we joined the Church—we are tired of the restrictions we have to follow."

(A wife to her husband): "I get discouraged when I read the Church magazines. Always more to do! How does one ever measure up?"

(A student who is not a member of the Church to his Book of Mormon teacher at BYU): "People in this religion are tied down. They can't do anything to have fun. People just do not want to be this restricted."

Satan would deliberately and cleverly pervert our perspectives and attitude about these gifts called commandments. For the Church member, "pressing forward" then turns into a discouraging walk.

Five Principles

Following are five positive principles concerning obedience to God's commandments that we can ponder and teach to our families:

1. *Commandments come from an exalted and perfected father.* The commandments are the greatest safeguards that Father in Heaven has given his children to help them in their quest to regain his presence. Our God is wise, kind, just, merciful, patient, and long-suffering. In addition to these characteristics he knows all things, and because he knows the beginning from the end his plans for the salvation of his children cannot be frustrated. Most of all he is a god of love. He holds all attributes in perfection. What he does for his children is right in all cases; he makes no mistakes. His motivation is "to bring to pass the immortality and eternal life of man" (Moses 1:39). His fatherhood is perfected. Those who will achieve eternal life are those who have lent their hearts to his wisdom and hearkened to his counsel.

Bearing these two thoughts in mind: (1) the fatherhood of God, and (2) his perfected state, it is inconceivable that God would issue any directive that would be abusive, or any mandate to dominate unrighteously. A demonstration of his power and dominion would be purposeful, aligned with his perfections and aimed at the welfare of his offspring. Jesus said: "Or what man is there of you, whom if his son ask bread, will he give him a stone? Or if he ask a fish, will he give him a serpent? If ye then, being evil, know how to give good gifts unto your children, how much more shall your Father which is in heaven give good things to them that ask him?" (Matthew 7:9–11.)

Commandments, therefore, are gifts from a loving Father to his children; tools to help us progress; rules that secure safety; laws that provide freedom. In speaking to the Jews on one occasion, Jesus said: "If ye continue in my word, then are ye my disciples indeed; and ye shall know the truth, and the truth shall make you *free*" (John 8:31-32; italics added).

To continue in his word is to be obedient to his truth. The promised blessing is freedom—freedom to reach the measure of our intended creation; to be reunited with God and Jesus Christ.

2. *Commandments are similar to roadsigns that ensure safe passage.* In this life we have roadsigns or signposts. Some simply read "STOP." These are to be obeyed. If they are not, immediate negative consequences may result. Other familiar signs read: Yield; Railroad Crossing; Danger, High Voltage; Caution; Watch for Falling Rocks; Slippery When Wet; Watch for Animals. Once while driving from Provo to Arizona I must have either missed, or didn't pay attention to the sign warning me to watch for deer between particular points. At one o'clock in the morning, while traveling at fifty-five miles per hour, I struck a very large buck and terminated his life, at the same time putting the fan through the radiator of my car.

As the Book of Mormon mentions, is there not a "type" or "shadow" in this experience? Just as we have roadsigns that safely direct our daily lives, our Heavenly Father has given his children a whole additional set of roadsigns called commandments. As roadsigns direct, guide, and provide safe passage, so do these guideposts found in the Church.

Commandment signs might read: Come and Be Baptized; Receive the Holy Ghost; Repent; Have Family Prayer; Love Your Wife, Love Your Husband; Attend Your Church Meetings; STOP—Stay Chaste; Spiritual Death Ahead; CAUTION: R, X, and Some PG Movies—Filth and Pollution; No Detour; One Way Only—Temple Marriage.

With this perspective on commandments our own attitude changes, as well as our missionary approach. To the baptismal candidate we say: "Yes, be sure you know what you are getting into when you join the Church. We want you to know you will be blessed with a whole additional set of safeguards, specifically designed for your well-being." We would not tell our investigating friend that if he joins the Church he cannot go fishing on Sunday anymore; that invites a negative view, a taking away of something. Instead, we could tell him that the gospel will give him the opportunity to observe the holy Sabbath; that as he does this his life, and the life of his family, will be richer, fuller, and happier than ever before. To those who feel that it is sometimes hard to be a member of the Church we say, "Wouldn't it be much harder not being a member of the Church? Would you like to go around curves or steep cliffs without the aid of a sign warning you of icy or slippery roads?" What a blessing are these additional signs. Church members are not perfect, but isn't trying our best to obey all the signs, and sometimes getting a little frustrated, better than having no signs at all? Which sign or safeguard would we be willing to give up?

If you were to go on a long journey in an automobile, would you risk having bald tires, a weak battery, or a faulty transmission? No; you would not leave without the necessary parts to make it safely to your destination. If our relatives are in New York, we don't want to settle for going only as far east as Ohio. If our Father is in the celestial kingdom, we do not want to stop somewhere short of that destination. The commandments of God are the safeguards that help us press on successfully to our eternal home.

During my stay at the Brigham Young University—Hawaii campus, part of my duties included teaching the surfing class. At the beginning of the course I taught the students about hazardous currents and about areas of safe passage called channels. Channels are areas or passageways surfers paddle out through because they are relatively wave-free. One day a student of mine was having

extreme difficulty in trying to paddle out through the surf.
I called her name and signalled with my hand for her to follow me through the channel. She ignored my invitation
and continued to struggle. After ten to fifteen minutes with
no progress her struggle turned into complete frustration. I
could read her lips, which uttered unrepeatable words.

In reality, Heavenly Father is saying the same thing to
us with his commandments: "Paddle over here!" The one
who created the territory, who made the straight and narrow path, knows where the bad currents are and wants to
guide us away from them to a safe port.

So when we get tired and discouraged along the way
because the standard seems to be too high, when giving up
begins to seem the easier route, we need to remember the
perspective that the commandments of God are directive
signs beckoning us to safe passage.

3. *God's commandments are the necessary directions
on the gospel map.* Before embarking on a journey, a traveler examines his map and circles his destination. He notes
the important highways and marks the essential turnoffs.
Arrival at the designated spot is dependent on his ability to
follow the map.

When an investigator takes the missionary lessons, he
is given the gospel map. The end of the road is eternal life,
life with God the Father and Jesus Christ. The beginning
of the journey is baptism. The gospel package includes all
that one needs to know to achieve this destination, plus the
support system necessary to increase the likelihood of success. The commandments are the necessary directions as
to the highways and turns. Obviously, rejection of these
directions results in arrival at a different destination than
intended. There is no compulsion to accept the destination
or the map—people decide voluntarily where they will go.

With this thought in mind, to say it is foolish to follow a
prescribed course of moral conduct is to say it is foolish to
have a map when traveling. Not all roads lead to the same
destination. No one who accepts and follows a telestial

map will find the celestial kingdom, any more than two people starting at Texas, one going east, and one north, will both end up in New York. Rejecting the commandments of God is like rejecting the requirement to wear the parachute when jumping from a plane: the false sense of freedom is abruptly interrupted upon impact.

Insurance salesmen are usually armed with several plans. The customer is not forced to accept Plan A over Plan B. He voluntarily selects which plan will yield particular benefits when the policy comes due. It is absolutely requisite that he follow the terms of the contract—breaking the contract ends the company's obligation to pay benefits.

4. *Obedience to the commandments produces faith and hope.* When an individual aligns his conduct with his belief in the gospel he is exercising faith. Faith is rewarded with a confirmation regarding the correctness of the path taken—"signs shall follow them that believe" (Ether 4: 18). While speaking to a group of disbelieving Jews, Jesus said, "If any man will do his will, he shall know of the doctrine, whether it be of God, or whether I speak of myself" (John 7:17). In other words, a knowledge or witness of the truth of a gospel principle can be obtained by living the principle or being obedient to the commandment. Alma invited the Zoramites to "exercise a particle of faith" and "experiment" on his words. He compared the gospel to a seed and taught that one could discern if the seed was a good seed or a "true seed" by whether, after experimentation, it grew. The growth could be felt as swelling motions within. (See Alma 32:27, 28.) Undoubtedly, Alma was referring to the *witness* of the Holy Ghost *confirming* truth after the *exercise* of faith in planting the seed.

Faith and hope are inseparably connected. We hope for eternal life and qualify for that hope with individual faithfulness. Without obedience there is no faith; and without faith there is no power to achieve salvation. One cannot hope for something one is not actively seeking. Without faith there would be no obedience to gospel principles which would enable one to rightfully lay claim to a hope for salvation.

If a person were required to take an advanced chemistry test without previous study, he would have little hope of passing it. However, if he knew what to study, and had the time to learn the material, the hope of passing would transfer into an expectation of success. In the gospel, obedience to the commandments produces faith along with a hope that develops into a confident expectation of the eventual enjoyment of eternal life.

Again using the analogy of the traveler, if a person were to travel to a destination he had never been to before, he would rely heavily on a map. Following directions during the trip would keep the traveler on course. Although he would never see the final destination until he arrived, a hope of success would increase as the roadsigns continued to show the name of the desired route and a decrease in the number of miles left to travel. In life we travel by faith, following the gospel map. Obedience to the commandments represents the necessary turns. Along the way Heavenly Father rewards our faith with "signs," or witnesses, that "all is well," and if we continue on course it will be only a matter of time before we reach the destination: Zion, the city of our God.

Hope flows from faith, which is produced by obedience to the commandments. This hope can sustain travelers through the driest of deserts and the roughest roads life can produce. The opposite of hope is despair. Moroni clearly identified the causal factor which destroys faith and extinguishes hope: "And if ye have no hope ye must needs be in despair; and despair cometh because of iniquity" (Moroni 10:22).

5. *Commandments come from commanders.* Perhaps the difficulty for some people is the word *commandment.* It connotes unrighteous dominion or exercising authority over another. This thought activates our reflex for freedom, and rebellion follows. We must remember that com-

mandments *come from commanders*. What would an army do without a chief commander who, with confidence and experience, could lead them in the heat of battle? What would happen to a ship tossed between jagged coral without a skillful captain who knows the deep channel from the shallow reef? There is nothing grievous about receiving directions from a commander, especially when our commander is God. In the heat of our personal battles, stormy seas, and parched deserts we can "look to God" and be assured of victory. Defeat is unthinkable when one considers the character, attributes, power, and authority of the one who is "captain of their souls."

Consider the Wisdom of Each Commandment

With the aid of computers to analyze statistics, football teams can chart the tendencies of their opponents. When the opposition shows a particular formation, the quarterback and the defensive captain adjust according to predetermined strategy. They can act upon the situational changes from well-considered plans. They are not slow to react because they have already programmed themselves to carry out their responsibilities.

Similarly, knowledge of the purposes and wisdom behind each of God's commandments, accumulated through study, obedience, and prayer, can provide a storehouse of strong ammunition to combat temptation. This causes us to act from predetermined plans. Realizing the blessings of obedience makes disobedience totally illogical.

Consider the wisdom of the United States Constitution or the individual laws set up within the areas we live. What situation necessitated the law? For example, many states have passed a law requiring the use of car seats for infants. Statistics and experience show that unrestricted infants get killed in accidents that otherwise would have been minor. In the same way, Father in Heaven and Jesus Christ, the creators of our situation, know statistics better than anyone. They know the causal factors of failure and they know what brings progress and success on the path to eternal life. Their instructions, therefore, are all-purposeful to the end that all who will stay within the guidelines set may obtain the promised blessings.

An interesting challenge can be set up as follows: Make three columns on a piece of paper. In the left column list all the commandments you can think of. In the next column list the blessings or benefits of obedience. In the last column list the disadvantages of obedience. You then have a paper with each commandment listed, along with a positive and a negative column. Ponder over your answers. If you have done this honestly and sincerely the results will be at least twofold. As the hymn indicates, you will come to understand how gentle God's commands are, and you will know how kind his precepts are.

Perspective and Understanding

A major theme in the Book of Mormon is "inasmuch as ye shall keep [the] commandments, ye shall prosper . . ." (1 Nephi 2:20). The obedience of Lehi's family enabled them to find the land promised to their posterity as an everlasting "inheritance" (see 2 Nephi 1:5). Lehi's wilderness sojourn can be seen as a symbol of man's journey through the wilderness of life. Obedience to the commandments will bring each of God's children to a "far better land of promise" (Alma 37:45), an inheritance reserved for the meek, or those willing to submit, as did Jesus, to the will of the Eternal Father.

In opposition to this idea comes the voice of the atheist; like Korihor of old he proclaims Christians to be in bondage, yoked by the foolish traditions of a belief in Christ. To him, commandments are used by priests to usurp power over people who would otherwise be free to prosper "according to [their] genius" and conquer "according to [their] strength." Sin and guilt are products of the mind, truth is relative, there is no divine standard to offend, and people should be taught to "lift up their heads," for "whatsoever a man did was no crime." The resultant attitude of the acceptance of this philosophy is that individuals should live to "eat, drink, and be merry," for "when a man is dead, that is the end thereof." (Alma 30:13–18.)

A correct perspective and a deepened understanding of the nature and purposes of God's commands can strengthen us against the onslaught of clever and persistent arguments that pit the humble followers of Christ against those of the world who proclaim freedom to be a life with limited moral restraint.

9

Power Through Obedience

One day I was sitting in the library looking through my journal when I found a group picture of the ward of which I had been bishop. I started on row one and went through the picture face by face, and I was left with a singular impression: everyone has problems. I do not think I found one person who did not have some concern—either pressing, recently resolved, or a new one developing. The problems varied; morality, parents, grades, language, contention with a friend, dishonesty, poor employment, the marriage decision, self-image, finances, fear, rejection, homesickness, illness, depression, and guilt. In the picture everyone was smiling and giving the impression that they were in total control of their lives.

As a bishop, I learned that some people are entangled in habits that for years have caused a lack of self-confidence and self-worth, and a denial of blessings they could have received. The formula to achieve the power necessary to overcome every obstacle that we encounter is stated very simply in one of our hymns: "Do what is right; let the consequence follow."

Cause-and-Effect Blessings

The dictionary defines a consequence as a result of an action or process; an outcome or effect. My wife makes the most wonderful spaghetti. A combination of the right ingredients in the bowls and pans plus the right time and temperature in the cooking produces a consequence that is delightful to the taste. If the recipe is followed meticulously, the taste never varies; the results are sure, and experience through repetition brings confidence to the cook.

Just as there are cause-and-effect relationships in our temporal existence, they also occur in spiritual things. I have found this cause-and-effect relationship very consistent, so much so that I have come to rely upon it.

The scriptures are full of statements showing these relationships:

> Whatsoever a man soweth, that shall he also reap (Galatians 6:7).

> Cast thy bread upon the waters: for thou shalt find it after many days (Ecclesiastes 11:1).

> Pride goeth before . . . a fall (Proverbs 16:18).

> Inasmuch as ye shall keep my commandments, ye shall prosper (1 Nephi 2:20).

> Because of the rock upon which ye are built (Christ), [you] cannot fall (Helaman 5:12).

> Ask, and it shall be given you (Matthew 7:7).

> He that believeth and is baptized shall be saved (Ether 4:18).

> Come unto me . . . and I will give you rest (Matthew 11:28).

This cause-and-effect system of blessings operates under the umbrella of faith in the Lord Jesus Christ. Jesus said, ''If any man will *do* his [Heavenly Father's] will, he shall *know* of the doctrine, whether it be of God, or whether I speak of myself'' (John 7:17; italics added).

Doing is the key, *knowing* is the consequence. Our obedience to the spiritual formulas given by the Savior will always produce the prophesied results.

What does it mean to ''do what is right?'' In the spiritual context we ''do right'' when we are:

1. Obeying the standards and principles taught in the scriptures.
2. Obeying the standards taught by the living prophets.
3. Obeying personal revelation given by the light of Christ, or through the gift of the Holy Ghost.

''Doing right'' is central to overcoming any and every problem that will arise on the path to eternal life. By being obedient we show our faith in Jesus Christ. When we exercise our faith in this manner we place ourselves in a position to receive the Lord's blessings. Jesus Christ is the answer — all ''right'' centers in him. Enos, the son of Nephi's brother Jacob, put himself in a position to receive his desired blessing through a broken heart and a contrite spirit, which compelled him to offer a mighty prayer all day and into the night. Finally, he heard a voice: ''Enos, thy sins are forgiven thee.'' Relieved, yet curious, Enos replied, ''Lord, how is it done?'' The answer shows the great consistency throughout the scriptures about the source of relief, strength, nourishment, and power: ''Because of thy faith in Christ.'' (Enos:2–8.)

During the second year of our Lord's ministry there was a woman who had had a physical difficulty for twelve years.

> And a woman having an issue of blood twelve years, which had spent all her living upon physicians, neither could be healed of any,

Came behind him, and touched the border of his garment: and immediately her issue of blood stanched.

And Jesus said, Who touched me? When all denied,
Peter and they that were with him said, Master, the multitude throng thee and press thee, and sayest thou, Who
touched me?

And Jesus said, Somebody hath touched me: for I per-
ceive that virtue is gone out of me.

And when the woman saw that she was not hid, she
came trembling, and falling down before him, she declared unto him before all the people for what cause she
had touched him, and how she was healed immediately.
(Luke 8:43–47.)

What was the cause of the healing effect on this
woman's life? What had she been doing earlier in the day
or the day before? Had she learned of Christ? Was her attitude that day one of curiosity? Was she a mere passerby,
or had she actively sought the Savior in faith? Verse 48
gives the Savior's reply: "Daughter, be of good comfort:
thy faith hath made thee whole; go in peace" (Luke 8:48).

It is instructive to note that the woman touched Jesus in
the *press* of the multitude. How could he discern the touch
of one amidst so many? It was the touch of faith that
caused the Savior to delay his journey to minister to the
needs of *one* who was afflicted.

How, then, can we, with our problems, be as the one
who touched Jesus and caused him to turn? Jesus said:
"Behold, I stand at the door, and knock: if any man hear
my voice, and open the door, I will come in to him, and
will sup with him, and he with me" (Revelation 3:20).

We are the ones who must take the initiative to open the
doors of our hearts to Jesus Christ. In the same sense, each
must personally reach for the hem of his garment to receive
the desired blessing. It is essential to remember that the
power behind the door or the garment is released not
through the mere professing of his name but through covenant and commitment to right things. This commitment

unleashes the powers of heaven and provides the particular blessings and gifts needed to overcome the hurdles which restrain us.

Stripling Warriors

Anciently in America there was a group of two thousand young men called, in the Book of Mormon, the stripling warriors. These young men were involved in several battles against their enemies, yet none of them were killed.

> But behold, to my great joy, there had not one soul of them fallen to the earth; yea, and they had fought as if with the strength of God; yea, never were men known to have fought with such miraculous strength; and with such mighty power did they fall upon the Lamanites, that they did frighten them; and for this cause did the Lamanites deliver themselves up as prisoners of war (Alma 56:56).

What act preceded the consequence of power among this group of young men? Perhaps a description of their characters, as stated scripturally, would give us a clue:

> They were men who were true at all times in whatsoever thing they were entrusted (Alma 53:20).

> They were men of truth and soberness, for they had been taught to keep the commandments of God and to walk uprightly before him (Alma 53:21).

> They had been taught . . . if they did not doubt, God would deliver them (Alma 56:47).

> Their minds are firm, and they do put their trust in God continually (Alma 57:27).

> They are strict to remember the Lord their God from day to day; yea, they do observe to keep his statutes, and his judgments, and his commandments continually (Alma 58:40).

If we want to have power and unity in our lives and in our families, perhaps the attributes that these young men possessed can be an example for us.

There is no power in hypocrisy. I played for some years on collegiate church-school volleyball teams. Although a team may possess players who have great skill, it has been my experience that the lack of personal integrity of individual team members weakens team unity and can negatively affect overall performance.

One year I played on a Church College of Hawaii team which could be described as a team of stripling warriors. We decided to do everything possible to promote unity and to properly represent our school and Church. In effect, we became our brothers' keepers. The regular season was filled with some very bad play, hard work, some better play, more hard work, and a unique closeness among the players. Our goal was to peak at the NAIA National Tournament in Iowa.

Our first match at the Nationals that year was against Chicago. We lost the first two games, then won the next three. We lost in the semifinals, which sent us to the losers' bracket. We won the finals of the losers' bracket, which put us in the finals of the tournament.

It was 5:20 P.M. and we were sitting around at the hotel waiting for the match and anticipating our chance to be champions. As I was lying on my bed thinking about our season—the hard work, the unity, the principles we had dedicated ourselves to, and, most of all, the upcoming game—the Spirit made it known to me that we would win our match. I sat up, got out a piece of paper, and wrote down the experience. I concluded my statement by writing that all Hawaii would be proud of us because we had represented ourselves well as Church members, athletes, and men. I signed it with a "congratulations," sealed it in an envelope, and tucked it away. I couldn't wait to get to the arena! The team we faced in the finals was the host school,

Graceland College. Graceland, a private school, is run by the Reorganized Church of Jesus Christ of Latter Day Saints. The saying went out that the church of the winner would be declared the true church!

The arena was full of noisy fans, all rooting for Graceland. Every time we made an error or Graceland did something good, the crowd screamed. We lost the first game in the best-of-three match.

We went behind six to four in the second game before breaking it open and winning 15–8. I was sure that the third game would be easier; in this final game, however, the rallies were long and the points were hard to get. With the score tied at eight someone tripped the lights, and they were the type that take ten minutes to come back on. This added to the tension and the anticipation of both the players and the fans. Play finally resumed and the score went to Graceland–11, Church College–9. Then the scorekeeper called a time-out and declared that he had made a mistake; and he changed the score from 11–9 to 12–8, Graceland.

I went to argue, but with no success. The score went to 14–11, Graceland—one more point and Graceland would win the championship. The crowd was wild and the noise reflected their anticipation of victory. We got the ball back, and it was my serve. I remember looking up to the ceiling of the dome and saying to myself, "You sure are making it tough for us, Lord."

The serve was a skyball, which is a high serve. A player called for it and then made a bad pass out-of-bounds—14–12. Then another skyball serve, and the Graceland players yelled "Out!" The ball bounced on the line—14–13. The next serve was a line drive serve which hit one of their players in the chest—14–14.

There were no more time-outs. We lost the ball, got it back, made the final two points, and won the National Championship. We were crying because we had won, they were crying because they had lost, and the crowd didn't know what to do. Our team circled up and we performed a Fijian war chant. The crowd gave us a standing ovation.

After we had carried each other around on our shoulders, and after the awards banquet, and after generally going crazy for awhile, we went back to the hotel and knelt down for team prayer. I then read to the team the congratulatory note I had written before the game. Several players mentioned that they had felt the same way as I had before the match. To the team, the year meant much more than a come back victory in an important tournament.

I do not believe that the Lord affects the outcome of athletic contests. The point is not whether we won or lost. It is that when we needed to reach down within ourselves there was substance to draw from. Our discipline to observe correct principles resulted in team unity and produced the strength and power to rise to our potentials during the time of need. Likewise in life, obedience creates a storehouse of strength within our souls to be called upon when needed to endure hardships, personal tragedy, and periods in which moving forward seems almost impossible.

Positive Ways to Overcome Sorrow, Disappointment, and Depression

Throughout my years as a religious educator I have had many interviews with students who were having difficulty in coping with very hard situations: divorce, the infidelity of a parent, cancer, death, and so on. Whatever the causal factor of discouragement or depression, the suffering individual is often unable to function. Appetite fades, sleep is difficult, and the mental stress is almost unbearable. Sometimes medical testing and psychiatric counseling are necessary.

Sorrow is a natural, healthy, and sometimes productive response to disappointments in life. For example: "Godly sorrow worketh repentance to salvation" (2 Corinthians 7:10). In many cases there needs to be a time of mourning to really let go of, or to gain a release from, the problem. Repression of feelings will take its toll on us and can be the cause of recurring guilt, sorrow, or depression over past issues that should have been resolved. A period of mourning allows introspection, emotional release, and a time to regroup our powers.

When sorrow or disappointment leads to discouragement or lingering, unproductive depression one must fight the desire to be alone and to just sit and think about the situation. Being busy is great medicine for the depressed. So often the spirit is rejuvenated when we become "actively engaged" in a positive activity.

When problems are complex and a multitude of things need to be resolved, it is common to feel overwhelmed. Being overwhelmed (not knowing what to do because there is so much that is wrong) can paralyze people into doing nothing. I taught tennis at BYU—Hawaii and I soon learned that if I gave too much instruction the student would "tie up." The brain can only process so much information. If I told the student all he needed to know to hit the forehand stroke before throwing him the ball, his first trials were miserable attempts. A player cannot concentrate on all the instruction and also focus on the ball. I discovered very quickly that I needed to give the students one key at a time and then let them focus on that key. It is the same with our problems. We cannot solve everything overnight; it is best to take one concern at a time and put the others on the shelf for a time. They can then be pulled out when it is time for them to be worked on. In this way people can work through their problems.

The great prophet Nephi was depressed with the fact that his own brothers had become his enemies. Laman and Lemuel had tried to kill him several times. In great sorrow Nephi poured out his soul: "O wretched man that I am! Yea, my heart sorroweth because of my flesh; my soul grieveth because of mine iniquities. I am encompassed about, because of the temptations and the sins which do so easily beset me. And when I desire to rejoice, my heart groaneth because of my sins; nevertheless, I know in whom I have trusted.'' (2 Nephi 4:17-19.)

The remaining verses of the chapter reveal the steps Nephi used to overcome his feelings of despair. The first thing he did was to count his blessings (see verses 20-25). He then reasoned with himself: ''O then, if I have seen so great things . . . why should my heart weep and my soul linger in the valley of sorrow, and my flesh waste away, and my strength slacken, because of mine afflictions?'' (verse 26). After reasoning with himself Nephi commanded himself: ''Awake, my soul! No longer droop in sin. Rejoice, O my heart, and give place no more for the enemy of my soul.'' (verse 28.) Finally, to receive help in keeping his commitment to ''awake,'' Nephi prays to the Lord for strength (see verses 31-34).

The formula is simple: Count the blessings we have, letting the counting produce a feeling of gratitude, which then produces a desire to get up and do something about the problem. As we go forward with the plan to endure, we must plead with the Lord for the help necessary to be successful. When Nephi broke his bow in the wilderness, everyone, including father Lehi, murmured. How did Nephi solve the problem? He simply went out and made another bow. We all break our ''bows'' in life. Whether the break is a professional setback, an illness, failing a test, falling into sin, or some other failure, the solution is to ''awake'' and apply the principle applicable to correcting the problem.

In the October 1975 general conference, President Ezra Taft Benson listed several ways to help deal with sorrow, disappointment, and depression. President Benson's suggestions included the importance of prayer, fasting, and reading the scriptures. He also stressed the value of good friendships, inspiring music, priesthood blessings, service, setting goals, and taking care of one's personal health.

Concerning the trials that come into our lives, President Benson said: "There are times when you simply have to righteously hang on and outlast the devil until his depressive spirit leaves you. . . . While you are going through your trial, you can recall your past victories and count the blessings that you do have with a sure hope of greater ones to follow if you are faithful."[1]

The Lord is always faithful in keeping his promises. When we do right, according to his own words he is bound to recognize and reward the faith shown. Often there is concern over the Lord's timing in administering his blessings. Faithful prophets have died in dungeons. Alma and Amulek prayed, yet remained in chains until the last wicked priest had smitten them on their cheeks. Prayers are always answered, but perhaps not according to "our will" or our own personal time schedule. The woman wearied the physicians for twelve years; the brother of Jared had to climb the mountain and melt out of rock and then polish twelve stones; Nephi and his brothers had to go back to Laban's house three times before obtaining the brass plates. We must use our minds, efforts, and agency.

How long will it be before we receive a promised blessing, an answer, or relief? The answer is, "As long as it takes." We are the pupils; God is the Father and teacher. Pupils do not set the blessing clock; it is adjusted and set by the teacher according to a schedule most apt to encourage us to reach for our divine potential. What, then, are we to know as students? The principle is that good will be restored to that which is good; righteousness for that which is righteous; and mercy for that which is merciful (see Alma 41:13).

Hang on as long as it takes, for surely our God is God; and if he can open the Red Sea, translate an ancient city, or bring Lazarus's spirit back to his decaying body, he can deliver us in due season if we "faint not" (see Galatians 6:9).

10

Decisions for Righteousness

The choice to be righteous is a deliberate seeking and selecting of decisions that will contribute to our progress and make it possible to retain the Holy Ghost as a companion. There are decisions that have spiritual impact, and there are those which have no right or wrong choices, in which it simply is a matter of preference. In a moral or religious sense there are right choices that are absolute and eternal as well as choices that are unquestionably wrong.

This sounds very elementary, yet the impact on one's life would be monumental if one would face decision making by asking the questions: Is it right? Will this course of action or thought please or displease Heavenly Father? How do I feel about it? Is justification or rationalization affecting my ability to see the real issue?

People often make their own gray areas and create their own confusion when they look at life with a worldly perspective rather than using gospel criteria. Mormon gives us the formula for distinguishing good from evil:

> For behold, the Spirit of Christ is given to every man, that he may know good from evil; wherefore, I show unto

you the way to judge; for every thing which inviteth to do good, and to persuade to believe in Christ, is sent forth by the power and gift of Christ; wherefore ye may know with a perfect knowledge it is of God.

But whatsoever thing persuadeth men to do evil, and believe not in Christ, and deny him, and serve not God, then ye may know with a perfect knowledge it is of the devil; for after this manner doth the devil work, for he persuadeth no man to do good, no, not one; neither do his angels; neither do they who subject themselves unto him. (Moroni 7:16–17.)

Multiple theaters have become popular throughout the United States. A moviegoer can approach the marquee, review what is playing at the different theaters, and choose which movie to see.

We could compare our daily choices to a multiple theatre. Perhaps the sign on one marquee would read: "Disciples of the Celestial Kingdom Enter Here." Underneath it would state: "You inherit all things." Looking toward another theatre you would read: "Disciples of the Telestial Kingdom." Underneath is the description: "You lose your birthright. You get nothing in comparison." Still another would read: "Disciples of the Terrestrial Kingdom." Perhaps the description would say: "You gain some things, but you eternally lose the greater blessings."

We would then approach the individual selling tickets. This person represents agency. We select the direction and agency will give us the ticket of our choice. Which theatre would we choose to enter? Obviously, with the consequences so clearly visible, there would be no difficulty in making our decision. In reality, however, perhaps too often we select activities and thoughts of a terrestrial and telestial nature rather than activities and thoughts which are proper to a person whose goal is clearly the celestial kingdom.

Is it too idealistic to view our decisions, our conversations, our associations, what we allow to come into our minds, by the standard: "What would Jesus have me do?"

The story is told of an All-American basketball player who was asked on national television to tell what he ascribed his great success to. His reply was immediate: "Batman." The commentator was taken aback, and asked him to explain. The star player continued by stating that ever since he was a boy he had collected and read all the Batman comic books and detective stories he could find. In addition, he had seen all of the Batman television episodes and cartoons. The commentator was still puzzled. "It is really quite simple," the athlete continued. "When I'm in a game and the going is tough and someone passes me the ball, all I have to do is ask myself one question—'What would Batman do?' "

As disciples of Jesus Christ, we can learn from this example. The response would be significant if we would say to ourselves: "I am consistently studying the life of Christ and his servants. Whenever the going gets tough, I will ask myself: 'What would Paul do? What would Alma do? What would Nephi do?' But most important, 'What would Jesus have me do?' "

Do what is right! President Spencer W. Kimball wrote, "A . . . power of discernment and perception comes to men as they become perfect and the impediments which obstruct spiritual vision are dissolved."[1] Satan would not have us clearly see the marquee that reads, "Telestial— you lose your birthright." He deceptively disguises his advertisements. President Kimball said:

> Whoever said that sin was not fun? Whoever claimed that Lucifer was not handsome, persuasive, easy, friendly? Whoever said that sin was unattractive, undesirable, or nauseating in its acceptance?
>
> Transgression wears elegant gowns and sparkling apparel. It is highly perfumed, has attractive features, a soft voice. It is found in educated circles and sophisticated groups. It provides sweet and comfortable luxuries. Sin is

easy and has a big company of bedfellows. It promises im-
munity from restrictions, temporary freedoms. It can mo-
mentarily satisfy hunger, thirst, desire, urges, passions,
wants, without immediately paying the price. But, it begins tiny and grows to monumental proportions. It grows
drop by drop, inch by inch.[2]

There is right and there is wrong; and doing right in-
creases our power to discern between the two.

The Book of Mormon: An Invitation to Choose

In speaking to his son Jacob, Lehi taught:

> Wherefore men are free according to the flesh; and all
> things are given them which are expedient unto man. And
> they are free to choose liberty and eternal life, through the
> great Mediator of all men, or to choose captivity and
> death, according to the captivity and power of the devil;
> for he seeketh that all men might be miserable like unto
> himself. (2 Nephi 2:27.)

The Book of Mormon is very plain in its identification
of choices which lead to everlasting happiness and choices
which lead to eternal misery. The events in the Book of
Mormon are cases in point which verify the consequences
of using one's agency to choose either Christ or Satan. For
example: the choices of Nephi and Sam versus the choices
made by Laman and Lemuel; the decision to hold to the
iron rod and press forward to the tree of life versus the decision to leave the path and enter the great and spacious
building which was symbolic of the world (see 1 Nephi 8).

When one reads the Book of Mormon with this thought
in mind, the contrasts seem to be everywhere: building
Zion through priesthood service versus serving self
through practicing priestcraft; hardening one's heart versus yielding one's heart to God; the gathering of Israel versus the scattering of Israel; being prospered and preserved

versus being cursed and afflicted. Fourth Nephi verses 1–18 records the righteousness of the Nephite nation after the visit of Jesus Christ. Verses 20 through 45 contain an entire list of wrong choices which led to the complete destruction of this people later. One cannot read the Book of Mormon with a sincere heart and remain ignorant of the choices that would eternally bless one's life.

Accompanying the many case studies which epitomize the end results of either choosing right or choosing wrong are the invitations by the prophets and the Lord himself for all people to choose the path leading to everlasting joy. Lehi counseled his sons to "look to the great Mediator . . . and choose eternal life, . . . And not choose eternal death" (2 Nephi 2:28–29). After quoting the allegory of Zenos, the prophet Jacob extended a charge to the people based on the knowledge he had just imparted. Jacob invited his listeners to "come with full purpose of heart, and cleave unto God. . . . And while his arm of mercy is extended towards you in the light of the day, harden not your hearts." (Jacob 6:5.)

Following the destruction in America that preceded the Savior's coming, Jesus said of those who had rejected his words, "How oft *would I* have gathered you as a hen gathereth her chickens . . . and ye would not." Then to those who were spared Jesus cautioned, "How oft *will I* gather you . . . if ye will repent and return unto me with full purpose of heart." (3 Nephi 20:5, 6; italics added.) Standing upon the walls of Zarahemla, Samuel the Lamanite told the assembled Nephites: "He hath given unto you that ye might know good from evil, and he hath given unto you that ye might choose life or death; and ye can do good and be restored unto that which is good . . . or ye can do evil, and have that which is evil restored unto you" (Helaman 14:31). It is clear that the teachings of the Book of Mormon invite us to make choices and reveal to us the consequences of those choices.

Passing Our Trials of Faith

One day a colleague of mine confided that he had discovered a helpful application concerning scriptures that speak about trials of faith. He defined faith as *knowing* the true Christ, having never *seen* him. He further explained that faith produces the *desire* to be like Christ and to do things his way. Therefore, when we have a trial of faith it is a trial of whether we will choose *his* way or whether we will choose to do it *our* way.

We can view life in this same manner. Each of us face trials of our faith daily. The trials vary, inasmuch as we are all susceptible to different temptations. For example, while being offered a cigarette might not constitute a trial or temptation to one, standing at the video store contemplating renting an R-rated movie that stars a favorite actor might. The key is to remember that we always have a choice, and that when temptation introduces an alternative to gospel standards we need to take the time to ask ourselves: The Lord's way or mine?

11

God Is Faithful

When I was in a supermarket one day a popular tabloid at the checkout stand caught my attention. On the front page it listed the new psychic predictions for the coming year. One prediction was that a well-known model would become the nation's first lady. I asked myself, "What if that really came true? What if 50 or 75 percent of these predictions came true?" Most likely the tabloid's subscription would triple and the foreseers would be famous.

The scriptures are filled with God's predictions, or prophecies given through his prophets. Heavenly Father has never been untrue in what he has promised. Whether he is speaking to nations or individuals, God has shown his faithfulness to his word.

For example, from Lehi's time to the days of Mormon the decree of God was that "inasmuch as ye shall keep the commandments of God ye shall prosper in the land;" and "inasmuch as ye will not keep the commandments of God ye shall be cut off from his presence" (Alma 36:30). The Book of Mormon gives its readers one thousand years of Nephite-Lamanite history which verify this divine pronouncement. Amaron, viewing the destruction of "the more wicked part of the Nephites," recorded:

> For the Lord would not suffer, after he had led them out of the land of Jerusalem and kept and preserved them from falling into the hands of their enemies, yea, *he would not suffer* that the words should not be verified, which he spake unto our fathers, saying that: Inasmuch as ye will not keep my commandments, ye shall not prosper in the land (Omni 1:6; italics added).

In a broader context, the Lord will not allow *any* of his words to fail or to be proven untrue. In preface to the revelations recorded in the Doctrine and Covenants, the Lord said: "What I . . . have spoken, I have spoken, and I excuse not myself; and though the heavens and the earth pass away, my word shall not pass away, but shall all be fulfilled" (D&C 1:38). What should it mean to us to know that God, by his very nature, is "bound" to keep his word to us if we keep our promises to him? (See D&C 82:10.) We do not have to worry about God being true to us. This knowledge frees us to work fully on our efforts to be true to him. Furthermore, knowing that God fulfills his words and promises enables us to develop the faith and trust necessary to truly become "as a child . . . willing to submit to all things which the Lord seeth fit to inflict upon [us], even as a child doth submit to his father" (Mosiah 3:19).

God Supports Us in Adversity

Adversity is part of life's terrain. It is present, in greater or lesser degrees, as each of us progresses. The prophet Alma taught his sons concerning the reliability of God in supporting the faithful during adversity:

> And I have been supported under trials and troubles of every kind, yea, and in all manner of afflictions; yea, God has delivered me from prison, and from bonds, and from

death; yea, and I do put my trust in him, and he will still deliver me (Alma 36:27).

From his own experiences Alma could bear testimony of the faithfulness of God. Those experiences then became anchors for Alma, which increased his trust in God.

The Lord is anxious to show his people that he will support them in their trials. Alma's followers entered the waters of baptism, making the covenant to "stand as witnesses of God at all times and in all things, and in all places" (Mosiah 18:9). The new converts received the opportunity to prove their sincerity when they were taken into bondage by the Lamanites and forbidden, upon the threat of death, to pray. The faithful prayed within their hearts.

> And . . . the voice of the Lord came to them in their afflictions, saying: Lift up your heads and be of good comfort, for I know of the covenant which ye have made unto me; and I will covenant with my people and deliver them out of bondage.
>
> And I will also ease the burdens which are put upon your shoulders, that even you cannot feel them upon your backs, even while you are in bondage; and this will I do that ye may stand as witnesses for me hereafter, and that ye may know of a surety that I, the Lord God, do visit my people in their afflictions. (Mosiah 24:13–14.)

The Lord was true to his promise. The Book of Mormon records that the Lord "did strengthen them that they could bear up their burdens with ease, and they did submit cheerfully and with patience to all the will of the Lord" (Mosiah 24:15). In consequence of their great faith and patience, "the voice of the Lord came unto them again, saying: Be of good comfort, for on the morrow I will deliver you out of bondage" (Mosiah 24:16).

In summary, the Lord allowed Alma's people to suffer affliction; the people continued to be faithful in affliction;

the Lord visited them in their afflictions and made their
burdens light; the people submitted cheerfully and with
patience to the will of the Lord; and revelation came prom-
ising deliverance. In this case it appears that the Lord
allowed this group of righteous Nephites to have this experience so that after their bondage ended they could testify
to others of God's supporting hand through the difficulties
of life.

Great lessons can be learned from this story. The Lord
knows our struggles and problems, and perhaps, as he did
with Alma's people, he allows us to show our faith and patience before the deliverance comes. Having made the covenant to be "witnesses of God at all times," we must remember that "all times" includes times of affliction as
well as times of ease. We can then become instruments in
the hands of God to influence others as we testify of his
assistance.

In every family there are times when everything seems
to go wrong. Many times afflictions come when we are
striving our hardest to do what is right. We feel like Joseph
Smith, who was in Liberty Jail when he asked, "Oh God,
where art thou?" (D&C 121:1).

Several years ago my wife contracted pnuemonia. She
coughed so much that she broke two ribs. At the same time
my son was having frequent and very severe asthma attacks, and my daughter was also ill. One evening while I
was at a bishopric meeting, my wife called saying that the
doctor had just phoned to say that my chest x-rays had revealed a tumor. I was to see a surgeon immediately.

When I returned to school and church after recovering
from the surgery, a student approached me and said,
"How do you figure, Bishop? You are doing all these
things for the Church, and look at you with that tumor!
Why did God let that happen?" I thought for a minute and
then replied: "Life is a school. The Lord didn't give me the
tumor—it was an unnatural cell growth. The Lord never
said we wouldn't have problems, but he did promise that
he would support us in our problems."

The Faithful Die and the Saints Suffer

The Book of Mormon contains the story of a group of righteous saints who were put to death because they refused to deny their testimonies. The wicked leaders of Ammonihah brought Alma and Amulek to the scene of martyrdom, where the followers of their teachings were being cast into a fire:

> And when Amulek saw the pains of the women and children who were consuming in the fire, he also was pained; and he said unto Alma: How can we witness this awful scene? Therefore let us stretch forth our hands, and exercise the power of God which is in us, and save them from the flames.
>
> But Alma said unto him: The Spirit constraineth me that I must not stretch forth mine hand; for behold the Lord receiveth them up unto himself, in glory; and he doth suffer that they may do this thing, or that the people may do this thing unto them, according to the hardness of their hearts, that the judgments which he shall exercise upon them in his wrath may be just; and the blood of the innocent shall stand as a witness against them, yea, and cry mightily against them at the last day. (Alma 14:10–11.)

Amulek was justifiably upset with the scene he was witnessing, but Alma taught him a great lesson that can be applicable to our own sufferings. Justice is not always available *in this life*; the Lord allows suffering at the hands of others so that justice might be meted out *in the life hereafter*. Alma taught that what we "send out shall return . . . again." It will be restored, "evil for evil . . . carnal for carnal . . . good for that which is good . . . just for that which is just." (Alma 41:15, 13.)

Being a member of the church Jesus established on the earth is no guarantee that life's tribulations will pass us by. In every stake in Zion there are incidents of death, disease, loss, and destruction. Men die in the prime of their lives, leaving behind widows and fatherless children. Children of tender ages contract cancer and die almost before their lives are begun. People who suffer blindness, deafness, paralysis, and chronic disease can be found everywhere. International tragedies and disasters are so commonplace that news of their happenings is quickly forgotten by those not touched directly. Wars are being fought in many nations by many good people who suffer and whose families suffer.

In the face of such trials, one commonly hears comments such as, "There must not be a Supreme Being. Otherwise, he would not allow these tragedies to occur." How does one reconcile the fact that, as the title of a popular book puts it, ". . . Bad Things Happen to Good People?" How does one face a crisis and continue on with one's faith intact?

In his book *Tragedy Versus Destiny* President Spencer W. Kimball addressed the fact that sometimes the righteous will die and the Saints will suffer. He spoke of the reality that no one really knows the answer to the question of what the Lord causes to happen in our lives and how much he permits. However, the Lord wisely allows us to have trials to overcome in order to fulfill the plan of salvation. President Kimball admonished us to look at the eternal perspective of time and to understand that being tested and learning to walk by faith are important components of the reason we came to earth. He said: "If all the sick for whom we prayed were healed, if all the righteous were protected and the wicked destroyed, the whole program of the Father would be annulled and the basic principle of the gospel, free agency, would be ended. No man would have to live by faith."[1]

If in the course of our lives we are called upon to suffer unrighteously; if judgment is not meted out in this life; if we feel tempted to "curse God and die" or to blame God for his lack of support—in any such circumstances it is crucial that we remember to look at mortality as but a few moments in eternity, and to gain an eternal perspective. God *is* faithful; he *does* support and uphold his own; and those who *do* endure to the end will eventually have all their questions answered. And all justice will be met.

Keep a Journal of Faith-Promoting Experiences

It would be helpful to keep in our journals our own "God is faithful" section. As we look back over our life and see that obedience has brought us blessings, we could write the experiences and stories down. Then, when we get tired on the road of life and need faith to move forward, we can open the book and see that our Heavenly Father is a perfect, consistent friend. He came through for us in the past; do we have any reason to doubt that he will do so now, or in the future?

In Galatians 6:9 we read: "And let us not be weary in well doing: for in due season we shall reap, if we faint not."

12

Remember, Remember

Toward the end of his writings in the Book of Mormon, Nephi exhorted his readers to "press forward, feasting on the words of Christ" (2 Nephi 31:20). There are many reasons why such a spiritual feast is vital. Consistent study of spiritual truths not only nourishes a person's soul at the time they are first encountered, but once stored they can later be retrieved during critical periods of personal need.

An example of this is the story of Alma the Younger, who, when recounting his conversion story to his son Helaman, said:

> And now, for three days and for three nights was I racked, even with the pains of a damned soul.
>
> And it came to pass that as I was thus racked with torment, while I was harrowed up by the memory of my many sins, behold, *I remembered also to have heard my father prophesy* unto the people concerning the coming of one Jesus Christ, a Son of God, to atone for the sins of the world.
>
> Now, as my mind caught hold upon this thought, I cried within my heart: O Jesus, thou Son of God, have

mercy on me, who am in the gall of bitterness, and am encircled about by the everlasting chains of death. (Alma 36:16–18; italics added.)

It was the remembering of the words spoken by his father about Jesus Christ and the Atonement that came to Alma as a solution in a time of spiritual crisis. Enos had a similar experience when he went into the forest to hunt beasts. He wrote:

Behold, I went to hunt beasts in the forests; *and the words which I had often heard my father speak concerning eternal life, and the joy of the saints, sunk deep into my heart.*

And my soul hungered; and I kneeled down before my Maker, and I cried unto him in mighty prayer and supplication for mine own soul; and all the day long did I cry unto him; yea, and when the night came I did still raise my voice high that it reached the heavens. (Enos 1:3–4; italics added.)

It was the "words" he remembered that motivated Enos to offer up a mighty prayer, which resulted in his obtaining a forgiveness of his sins.

In the story of the stripling warriors, Helaman questioned his band of two thousand young men as to whether they should assist Antipus in the war against the Lamanites. Helaman said: "My sons, will ye go against them to battle?" (Alma 56:44.) They responded: "Behold our God is with us, and he will not suffer that we should fall" (Alma 56:46). In describing their extraordinary faith to Captain Moroni, Helaman said that they had rehearsed to him the words of their mothers that "if they did not doubt, God would deliver them" (Alma 56:47). The remembered words of righteous mothers engendered the faith to fight and the miracle to survive the maturity of the Lamanite army.

As a nonmember of the Church, I attended BYU–Hawaii on a volleyball scholarship. At the close of the

semester our team boarded a bus for the airport en route to
the National Championships in Knoxville, Tennessee. The
bus made one stop at the home of the department chair-
man of Physical Education, who wanted to wish us well.
He got on the bus and began to deliver his "pep talk."
Then he walked up the aisle and sat down in the seat in
front of me. He looked at me and paused. During the si-
lence his eyes began to well up with tears, and finally he
spoke: "I want you to know that the things you learned
while at this school about the Church and the gospel are
true." He paused again, then looking at the rest of the
team he added, "That goes for the rest of you also."

Three years later I had occasion to remember his
words. Sitting alone in a small apartment in Santa Monica,
California, I reflected on my life and where I was going.
The words of the man on the bus filtered back to me and I
remembered what he had said and how it had touched me.
I realized that I wanted to be like this man. My courage
and resolve strengthened and I picked up the telephone
and dialed the local missionaries. The remembered words
were significant in bringing me into the Church.

One Sunday I attended a testimony meeting in the ward
in which my wife grew up. A man stood up and began to
rehearse his feelings of gratitude for the people of the
ward. He too was visiting that day, having grown up as a
member of this particular ward. He stated his appreciation
for the influence of the people there, his learning of the
gospel, and the significance of the ward in shaping his life.
He said: "I can still remember Brother Belnap standing at
this pulpit telling the story about his lost glasses." West
Belnap was my wife's father and he had passed away
almost twenty years previous to this occasion. The remembered story of the glasses was included in a paper he
wrote.

When I was a young man in the ninth grade, I pur-
chased my first pair of glasses. Shortly after this I went
fishing up South Fork. I fished up the river a good dis-

tance when it began to get dark, so I started to come back to our camp. I crossed the river, and as I did, I fell into the river. As I stood up I knew something was different, but I was unable to determine what it was. When I came back to the camp, I changed my clothing, and I went to clean my glasses; then I knew what was different. My glasses had fallen when I had fallen; I had lost them. I went back that night and attempted to find the glasses, I could not find them, although I looked hard for them. Finally I got on my knees and I prayed as my parents had taught me. I asked my Father in Heaven that I might find them. I told Him what a problem it was and how I needed them and that it was necessary. Something came over me and turned my body directly upstream, and I walked two or two and a half blocks along the side of the river, crossed through a fence, went out into the middle of the river and something directed my hand to the bottom of the river, and I came up with my glasses. I knew that God heard and answered prayers.[1]

I thought how meaningful it was that a boy heard a story, came back to the congregation as a mature adult, and in connection with his appreciation for the influence of these people recollected a story he had never forgotten. The remembered words of B. West Belnap had helped teach him, as a young man; that prayers are indeed heard and answered.

While attending a missionary farewell for an elderly widow I heard her appreciative son speak of his mother's influence: "I remember the stories my mother told me about living in Mexico. One time the Saints needed rain. The members fasted, and during stake conference it began to rain. Those types of things have always had an effect upon me. My mother was there—she witnessed it, and that testimony has always been with me."

The scriptures are replete with similar examples. It is clear that there is great value in filling our own storehouses with spiritual experiences, as well as in constructing environments which encourage spiritual learning for those we love. In the scriptures we read: "Train up a child in the way he should go: and when he is old, he will not depart from it" (Proverbs 22:6). The examples of Enos, Alma the Younger, and the stripling warriors teach us that children do indeed listen and learn from the spiritual training and experiences of their parents. Parents who desire that their children gain testimonies of their own and learn to transfer faith into an active attribute would do well to structure spiritual learning experiences that their children can listen to and collect in their own personal storehouses. Then, in times of crisis or decision-making, the Holy Ghost can perform in his function of calling up memory, and the remembered words will be helpful in effecting a righteous solution.

13

The Purpose of the Church

It is easy to feel overwhelmed when we consider all we Church members are required to know, believe, and do. The scriptures overflow with instructions and standards by which to judge our actions. In church we are constantly admonished to "choose the right," live the Word of Wisdom, study the scriptures, pray, pay our tithing, hold family home evening, do our home teaching, and make frequent visits to the temple. As we confront the challenge and view our performance, we often see a disparity between what we know and what we do.

Increased righteousness brings an increased portion of the Spirit. The Holy Ghost sensitizes us to sin, and under that influence we become aware of even more that we need to accomplish in our discipleship. Sometimes we hear righteous individuals say that if they were to die today they would be concerned for their salvation. This adds to our frustrations and doubts; how perfect do we need to be to inherit eternal life? Is Heavenly Father pushing us back with a multitude of commandments so, truly, there will be "few" that enter the final gate into the celestial kingdom?

Counsel from King Benjamin

King Benjamin gave us a list of things to consider (Mosiah chapter 4). He listed things we need to know, believe, do, remember, and teach if we would inherit eternal life.

Things we must know. We need to know of the goodness of God; the relative nothingness of fallen man; God's matchless love, and his wisdom, patience, and longsuffering; and the Atonement.

Things we must do. We must trust in the Lord; be diligent in keeping the commandments; continue in the faith even until the end of life; not have a mind to injure another; grow in the knowledge of the glory of him that created us; live peaceably; render to every man according to that which is his due; not allow our children to go hungry or naked, to transgress, or to serve the devil; succor those that stand in need of succor; administer of our substance unto him that stands in need; not turn away the beggar; return what we borrow; and retain a remission of sins.

Things we must believe. We must believe in God; that he created all things; that he has all wisdom and all power; and that man does not comprehend all the things the Lord comprehends. And we must believe that we need to repent, humble ourselves, and forsake our sins.

Things we must remember. We must remember to call on the Lord daily, and to stand steadfast in the faith.

Things we must teach. We must teach our children to walk in the ways of truth and soberness, and to love one another and serve one another.

King Benjamin finished his admonition with this caution:

> And finally, I cannot tell you all the things whereby ye may commit sin; for there are divers ways and means, even so many that I cannot number them.

But this much I can tell you, that if ye do not watch yourselves, and your thoughts, and your words, and your deeds, and observe the commandments of God, and continue in the faith of what ye have heard concerning the coming of our Lord, even unto the end of your lives, ye must perish. And now, O man, remember, and perish not. (Mosiah 4:29-30.)

How do we do all that is required of us and not get overwhelmed? King Benjamin suggested a key: "And see that all these things are done in wisdom and order; for it is not requisite that a man should run faster than he has strength. And again, it is expedient that he should be diligent, that thereby he might win the prize; therefore, all things must be done in order." (Mosiah 4:27.)

All that King Benjamin advised us to do must be done in order, with the stipulation that we not run faster than we have strength. Wisdom teaches that the road to perfection is a process of growth. This growth must be carefully ordered and balanced in order for us to achieve the depth and strength sufficient to sustain its continuance.

Activity in the Church Fosters Godlike Growth

Running faster than we have strength exhausts our resources and can drop us into personal valleys of weakness and discouragement. Sometimes even *finishing* the race is difficult when the pace is set beyond one's capacity to endure. The Church provides the order, or organization and balance, to "perfect the Saints." If one considers all one is required to do in the various programs within the Church, it is easy to see that activity in the Church provides a balanced, ordered growth towards perfection. For example, what do we have in the Church to help us fulfill King Benjamin's admonition to grow in the knowledge of God? We have priesthood meetings, sacrament meetings, Sunday School, Primary, institutes of religion, seminaries, firesides, general conferences, "Know Your Religion" series, education weeks, and so forth.

What do we have in the Church that helps retain a remission of sin? We have the opportunity to partake of the sacrament each week and thus renew the covenants we made at baptism.

What do we have in the Church that can help us learn to impart of our substance to others? We have tithing, fast offerings, budget, building funds, missionary funds, and opportunities to sacrifice our time by serving in the temple and working in a Church calling.

What do we have that can help us teach our children? We have the family home evening program, parents' firesides, Primary, Young Men and Young Women programs, Scouting, and so forth.

When we consider all these programs, we realize that everything is already in place to help us "grow" to heaven. In order to progress it is imperative that we be active in Heavenly Father's organization.

Must Our Growth Reach Perfection Before Death?

On the matter of how and when we may reach perfection Elder Bruce R. McConkie had this to say:

> As members of the Church, if we chart a course leading to eternal life; if we begin the processes of spiritual rebirth, and are going in the right direction; if we chart a course of sanctifying our souls, and degree by degree are going in that direction; and if we chart a course of becoming perfect, and, step by step and phase by phase, are perfecting our souls by overcoming the world, then it is absolutely guaranteed—there is no question whatever about it—we shall gain eternal life. Even though we have spiritual rebirth ahead of us, if we chart a course and follow it to the best of our ability in this life, then when we go out of this life we'll continue in exactly that same

course. We'll no longer be subject to the passions and the appetites of the flesh. We will have passed successfully the tests of this mortal probation and in due course we'll get the fulness of our Father's kingdom—and that means eternal life in his everlasting presence.

The Prophet told us that there are many things that people have to do, even after the grave, to work out their salvation. We're not going to be perfect the minute we die. But if we've charted a course, if our desires are right, if our appetites are curtailed and bridled, and if we believe in the Lord and are doing to the very best of our abilities what we ought to do, we'll go on to everlasting salvation, which is the fulness of eternal reward in our Father's kingdom.[1]

The Church—A System of Support

God's central aim is the salvation of his children. The design, therefore, of his organization is to maximize the possibility of obtaining salvation. The Church is God's organizational plan to increase the likelihood of the continued faithfulness and success of his children. Immersing oneself into divine programs, instituted by a divine being, will most certainly yield the intended results. The dramatic differences between life in and life out of the Church can be demonstrated when one counts the immediate additions to the life of a new convert.

Baptism into the Church brings an army of support into a person's life. Each of us must work out our own salvation, and therefore we personally are the central characters in our mortal drama. Heavenly Father, through his church, has given us a supporting cast whose specific commission is to watch over and care for the welfare of the souls of its members. Anciently, Moroni wrote about the Nephite church and explained the reasons for the "taking," or recording, of the names of newly baptized members of the Church:

> And after they had been received unto baptism, and were wrought upon and cleansed by the power of the Holy Ghost, they were numbered among the people of the church of Christ; and their names were taken, that they might be remembered and nourished by the good word of God, to keep them in the right way, to keep them continually watchful unto prayer, relying alone upon the merits of Christ, who was the author and the finisher of their faith.
>
> And the church did meet together oft, to fast and to pray, and to speak one with another concerning the welfare of their souls. (Moroni 6:4–5.)

The Church today is record-conscious for the same reasons that the Nephites were. After baptism, a person receives the help of home teachers, visiting teachers, an elder's quorum president, a Relief Society president, a stake president, and a bishop. All of these people are distinctly interested in the person's spiritual success. In fact, they have a direct "stewardship" to do all that is appropriately possible to help the new member stay faithful to the commitments made at baptism.

In addition to the Church leaders mentioned that have direct contact, the new member enjoys the guidance and inspiration of Apostles and prophets. These men are prophets, seers, and revelators who provide messages that are timely and essential.

Within the Church organization a convert enjoys many blessings, all correlated for his benefit, which were unavailable before he joined the Church. A member enjoying the fulness of the restored gospel has: the truth concerning where he came from, why he is here, and what lies beyond his mortal life; a correct understanding of Jesus Christ and his atoning mission; the gift of the Holy Ghost; the priesthood; marriage for time and all eternity; priesthood blessings; patriarchal blessings; additional books of scripture; general conference; a Church employment program; a social service program; a personal preparedness program; the family home evening program; and so forth.

Upon pondering the design of The Church of Jesus Christ of Latter-day Saints, one can see the great desire Heavenly Father has for his children to return to his presence. Cutting oneself off from the Church by becoming inactive is in effect cutting oneself off from gifts, privileges, and blessings—all of which bring us safety and joy as we strive to endure to the end.

Would an Indianapolis 500 race-car driver fire his pit crew before the big race? Extra fuel and repairs are required to achieve the five-hundred-mile distance. In the sports world coaches and trainers provide athletes with technical information and physical training, as well as emotional and motivational support, so they can continue toward the fulfillment of their goals. In hospitals, nurses and doctors work around the clock for the well-being of their patients. Without support we fail in so many things. While having our name on the Church records means we will be met by outstretched arms interested in our welfare, being active in the Church allows us to be lifted up by those arms. The end result of staying close to the Church is developing a character that makes one fit to enter the presence of God.

14

Prayer, Scripture, Sacrament

Almost twenty centuries ago Jesus organized his Church upon the earth and placed Apostles as the foundation. After the Crucifixion and the Resurrection, Jesus directed his Church through revelation to his appointed leaders. Because of wickedness and persecution the Apostles were killed, and the Lord removed his Church from the earth. No longer did the Church enjoy revelation to chosen leaders to direct its affairs. Lacking this continual guidance the kingdom of God on earth was swept by apostasy, and people "dwindled" in false beliefs.

Personal Prayer

One of the great messages we can learn from the apostasy is what happens to people when they no longer receive revelation from the Lord. The resulting condition is, as the apostle James stated, that they are "driven with the wind and tossed" (James 1:6). Just as the elimination of revelation produced a dramatic effect upon the Church, so can the elimination of personal prayer produce drastic results in an individual's life. Failure to pray cuts one off from God; in a sense, this is self-induced apostasy. When we pray sincerely we are recognizing that God is the source of all our blessings and that we are reliant upon him for all that is good in life. Without prayer we can drift in our priorities. Our hearts become set upon the world, and we treasure things that are material rather than spiritual. Without prayer a valuable immune system is removed; without this defense one is open to myriad spiritual diseases which are ravenously seeking an opportunity to breed.

Without personally inquiring of the Lord, Laman and Lemuel failed to understand the words of father Lehi (see 1 Nephi 15:8–9). They suffered in the wilderness because "they know not the dealings of that God who had created them" (1 Nephi 2:12). In Alma chapter thirty-one we read about the Zoramites. They had been Church members but had apostatized from the truth and developed a comfortable religion that supported their quest for material wealth and status. The Book of Mormon account details the false worship of the Zoramites and gives the key reason why they did not endure in righteousness:

> Now the Zoramites were dissenters from the Nephites; therefore they had had the word of God preached unto them.
>
> But they had fallen into great errors, for they would not observe to keep the commandments of God, and his statutes, according to the law of Moses.
>
> Neither would they observe the performances of the church, to continue in prayer and supplication to God daily, that they might not enter into temptation. (Alma 31:8–10.)

When people go away from the Church one of the first things to be eliminated from their lives is sincere personal prayer. On the other hand, it would be impossible to find a true follower of Christ whose life was devoid of prayer.

Prayer is the heart of discipleship. Prayer was the causal factor behind many of the great events and characters in the Book of Mormon. Lehi's prayers brought the command to leave Jerusalem, and thus saved his family from death or captivity at the hands of the Babylonians. Nephi's prayers brought testimony and assurance concerning the Lord's work through his father, Lehi. Enos's prayer (all day and into the night) brought forgiveness and a sweeping away of guilt. King Lamoni prostrated himself before the Lord in prayer and was taken away in the Spirit for three days. The prayer of Alma brought an angelic visitation to his wayward son. In prayer, King Mosiah received a promise concerning his sons' safety while they labored among the Lamanites. The prayer of the brother of Jared produced the revelation of Jesus Christ and help in lighting the barges that were to take his people across the great ocean. On another occasion, however, he was chastened by the Lord for three hours "because he remembered not to call upon the name of the Lord" (Ether 2:14).

To summarize, prayer is one of the keys to success in being able to endure to the end. If it is done sincerely it keeps our hearts in the right place and keeps us in touch with our Father in Heaven. People are not naturally hypocrites. Within everyone is the Light of Christ—we all have a conscience. To appear to be one thing and continue on a consistent basis to be something else is contrary to our spiritual makeup. Therefore it is hard to pray and yet live in sin. One of the first things that leaves our life when we are deviating from the path is prayer. From this fact we learn how important it is to keep praying no matter what. We must keep the channels open so that messages can get through when they are needed. Don't get discouraged when you feel prayers are bouncing off the ceiling in your bedroom. The Lord will always hear an earnest prayer. In any case it would seem that, in addition to the obvious purpose of communication, the act of prayer itself, regardless of the results or answers, is highly important to our spiritual growth. Reverence, humility, reliance, commitment, devotion, and pondering are all benefits of setting time aside to pray.

Great things from small means. One concept Nephi gave his readers concerning the Liahona Lehi received in the wilderness to guide his family was that "by small means the Lord can bring about great things" (1 Nephi 16:29). The Liahona itself was not large in size, yet the importance of its directive function meant the difference between perishing in the wilderness and "pressing forward" toward the group's prophetic destiny. The functioning of the instrument itself could be aptly described as simple. If Lehi's family were faithful and diligent, one of the spindles pointed in the direction that they were to go. If, however, they were "slothful, and forgot to exercise their faith and diligence . . . [the] marvelous works ceased, and they did not progress in their journey; therefore, they tarried in the wilderness . . . did not travel a direct course, and were afflicted with hunger and thirst, because of their transgressions" (Alma 37:41–42). Prayer is similar to the Liahona in that it opens up an avenue by which to receive directions for the guidance of our lives. To avoid perishing in the wilderness of life we, as Lehi's family did, must learn to give "heed and diligence" to this most important practice.

Prayer can have a powerful impact on our ability to endure to the end. For example, if a person prayed twice a day over the next fifty years of life, he would be in communication with Heavenly Father 36,524 times during those years. If each one of those prayers were one minute long he would pray more than 600 hours. If his prayers were extended to the small amount of five minutes twice a day, he would be in contact with Heavenly Father for something over 3,000 hours. One to five minutes twice a day is a small time commitment that could easily be extended. The point is, however, that sincere prayer can certainly increase our chance to receive "great things"; and the greatest of God's gifts is eternal life (see D&C 14:7).

Scripture Study

While in the wilderness Lehi had a dream that has significant implications for people living in any age. Central in his dream was a tree. A path located upon the banks of a river led to the tree. A rod of iron extended along the path the distance to the tree. Across the river, in sight of the tree, was a "great and spacious building." Hovering over the path to the tree was a thick mist of darkness.

Nephi inquired of the Lord regarding his father's dream and was shown the things Lehi saw and was given an interpretation of the symbols. The tree represented the love of God; the river, the depths of hell; the mists of darkness, the temptations of the devil; the iron rod, the word of God. The great and spacious building was a symbol of the pride and wisdom of the world.

Lehi also saw four groups of people in the dream. The groups represented the masses of people who populate the earth, and their varying responses to the gospel of Jesus Christ. The first group Lehi saw commenced on the path leading to the tree but were overcome by the mists. They lost sight of the tree, wandered off, and were lost in "strange paths." The second group "pressed" forward on the path, holding firmly to the iron rod. They survived the mists of darkness and made it to the tree, but while they were partaking of the fruit of the tree they looked across the river at the large building. The building was full of people who were mocking and pointing their fingers with scorn at those who were partaking of the fruit. The people at the tree reacted to the persecution from the "worldly" within the building and became ashamed and left the tree. Next, Lehi saw another group who had successfully arrived at the tree. They also noticed the people in the building, but they paid no attention to them. The fourth group did not start on the path but only sought place within the great building.

The conflict and the solution. The conflict portrayed in Lehi's dream was between the tree and the building; between those partaking of the love of God and those who love the world; between true happiness and momentary pleasure; between the humble and the proud; and between the doctrines of the kingdom of God and the false philosophies and doctrines of the world.

All of God's children are somewhere within Lehi's dream—everyone is moving in a direction determined by his thoughts, words, and actions. Success in life is dependent upon first *getting* to the tree, or coming to know God and feeling of his love, and then *staying* there, or enduring to the end. The key to meeting these two requirements, arriving and remaining at the tree, is in holding to the iron rod.

> But, to be short in writing, behold, he saw other multitudes pressing forward; and they came and caught hold of the end of the rod of iron; and they did press their way forward, continually holding fast to the rod of iron, until they came forth and fell down and partook of the fruit of the tree (1 Nephi 8:30).

It is important to note that in pressing forward the people continually held fast to the rod. This indicates a consistent and steady diet of the word of God. Nourishment must not be sporadic. It takes a consistent and persistent effort to stave off the clever and incessant allurement of the "great and spacious building."

In an epistle to Timothy, the Apostle Paul prophesied about conditions in the latter-days:

> This know also, that in the last days perilous times shall come.
>
> For men shall be lovers of their own selves, covetous, boasters, proud, blasphemers, disobedient to parents, unthankful, unholy,
>
> Without natural affection, trucebreakers, false accusers, incontinent, fierce, despisers of those that are good,
>
> Traitors, heady, highminded, lovers of pleasures more than lovers of God;
>
> Having a form of godliness, but denying the power thereof: from such turn away.

For of this sort are they which creep into houses, and lead captive silly women laden with sins, led away with divers lusts,

Ever learning, and never able to come to the knowledge of the truth. (2 Timothy 3:1–7.)

These conditions are similar to the many voices beckoning from the great and spacious building in Lehi's dream. They are contagious, and they correlate with the selfishness of the "me first" generation. In an address to religious educators in the Church Educational System, Elder Boyd K. Packer quoted Paul's prophecy and then made the following commentary:

While studying one day, I read to that point and sat pondering about all the evidence that now confirms every element in that prophecy. There was a mood of very deep gloom and foreboding, a very ominous feeling of frustration, almost futility. I glanced down the page, and one word stood out, not accidently I think. I read eagerly and then discovered that the apostle who had prophesied all that trouble had included in the same discourse the immunization against all of it.

Elder Packer then read from the scriptures:

But evil men and seducers shall wax worse and worse, deceiving, and being deceived.

But continue thou in the things which thou hast learned and hast been assured of, knowing of whom thou hast learned them;

And that from a child thou hast known the holy scriptures, which are able to make thee wise unto salvation through faith which is in Christ Jesus.

All scripture is given by inspiration of God, and is profitable for doctrine, for reproof, for correction, for instruction in righteousness:

That the man of God may be perfect, throughly furnished unto all good works. (2 Timothy 3:13–17.)

The word on the page that stood out to Elder Packer was scriptures. He concluded by saying: "Therein is contained the fulness of the everlasting gospel. Therein we find principles of truth that will resolve every confusion and every problem and every dilemma that will face the human family or any individual in it."[1]

With these thoughts in mind we can see that it is imperative for the disciple of Christ who is seeking to endure in righteousness throughout mortality to "feast on the words of Christ." The strengthening power of the word of God has a powerful effect upon people. Alma, in contemplating his mission to the Zoramites, reasoned: "And now, as the preaching of the word had a great tendency to lead the people to do that which was just—yea, it had had more powerful effect upon the minds of the people than the sword, or anything else, which had happened unto them—therefore Alma thought it was expedient that they should try the virtue of the word of God" (Alma 31:5).

As with prayer, reading the scriptures daily sets in place an immune system that repels the many and varied distractions attractively offered by modern society. Reading the scriptures puts us in contact with principles and precepts that, if obeyed, bring us closer to our Heavenly Father. In the scriptural stories we find consistent verification of God's word among his people. We learn what God expects of us and are given examples of those who applied gospel principles and those who rejected them. Likening these stories and their accompanying principles to our own lives fulfills a major objective of the written word. Moroni, in finishing his father's record, wrote the following:

> Condemn me not because of mine imperfection, neither my father, because of his imperfection, neither them who have written before him; but rather give thanks unto God that he hath made manifest unto you our imperfections, that ye may learn to be more wise than we have been (Mormon 9:31).

When we read the scriptures we store up knowledge that can be retrieved at critical periods of trial. It is similar to having the answer key before taking the exam. Another significant reason for reading the scriptures is that pondering the word of God can become a source of revelation. When we are struggling with problems, scripture reading and subsequent meditation provides the opportunity for the Spirit to "touch the eyes of our understanding." One of the greatest revelations in the Doctrine and Covenants (section 76, the "three degrees of glory" revelation) came as a result of reading and pondering a passage in the New Testament.

The shepherd's voice can be heard by his sheep through reading the words of Jesus Christ as recorded in the scriptures. In a revelation the Lord told Joseph Smith, Oliver Cowdery, and David Whitmer:

> These words are not of men nor of man, but of me; wherefore, you shall testify they are of me and not of man;
>
> For it is my voice which speaketh them unto you; . . . and by my power you can read them one to another; and save it were by my power you could not have them;
>
> Wherefore, you can testify that you have heard my voice, and know my words. (D&C 18:34–36.)

The Book of Mormon. The Lord, through the prophet President Ezra Taft Benson, has caught the attention of Latter-day Saints with repetitive admonitions regarding the blessings of and responsibilities toward the Book of Mormon. In the October 1986 general conference President Benson called God's gift of the Book of Mormon "more important than any of the inventions that have come out of the industrial and technological revolutions. This is a gift of greater value to mankind than even the many wonderful advances in modern medicine." He also said: "Every Latter-day Saint should make the study of [the Book of Mormon] a lifetime pursuit. Otherwise he is placing his soul in jeopardy and neglecting that which could give spiritual and intellectual unity to his whole life."[2]

In the same conference address President Benson said that there is a difference between one whose testimony is grounded in the Book of Mormon and one whose testimony is not.

The Prophet Joseph Smith, in speaking about the Book of Mormon, said that the record is the "keystone of our religion" and that "a man would get nearer to God by abiding its precepts, than by any other book."[3] One of the reasons, perhaps, that the Book of Mormon *is* the keystone of our religion is that all the doctrines and practices of the Church stand or fall on the truthfulness of the Book of Mormon. If the Book of Mormon is true, Joseph Smith was a true prophet and therefore the Church is true and all the additional works that proceeded forth from his hand are also divine. Having this testimony is an anchor in life against persecution from those who would deride and ridicule the concepts of restoration, prophets, revelation, and other gospel doctrines.

A student of mine shared the following letter that she had received from her sister. The letter illustrates the significant contribution the Book of Mormon can have in providing the type of testimony necessary to achieve the endurance required of each of us.

> It came as an incredible shock to me one day to find my testimony gone. I was studying in Paris at the age of nineteen. Culture shock, removal of familiar faces, places, and habits all took their toll. Discussions with "intellectual" associates left me grappling for words to support my religious beliefs. The Church seemed narrow and naive in the wake of the wide, wide world I was discovering.
>
> It was after many long weeks that I sat down one afternoon in my little Paris room and opened the Book of Mormon. Alma 32 says that the beginning of faith is desire. Did I desire to believe? I turned to 3 Nephi and began to read the account of the resurrected Christ visiting the Nephites. Suddenly I was struck with a realization. No man could have written this from his own mind! A rush of hope and light came pouring back into my hungry spirit. The Book of Mormon could not be explained away. It had a divine origin.

I mark that point as a profound beginning in my life. The testimony I have now has its roots in the warmth and hope of that moment. Twelve years have passed, during which time I have married in the temple, had five beautiful children, and served in many Church callings. I wonder where life would have taken me had I not reopened that wonderful book. I have heard it said that the Book of Mormon is the most correct book ever written. To me it was a lifesaver. I have a deep testimony in its truthfulness and in the existence of a loving God who speaks to prophets and all who will listen.

Another reason why the Book of Mormon is so important for us to study is its restorative role. In a vision, Nephi learned that when the Bible would first go forth from the Jews to the Gentiles the record would be pure and would contain the fulness of the gospel of the Lord. However, after it had gone forth to the Gentiles, many plain and precious parts and also many covenants would be taken away. This deliberate effort would be made in order to "pervert the right ways of the Lord, . . . [and] blind the eyes and harden the hearts of the children of men." Nephi then beheld that this incomplete record, missing precious parts and the plainness it once had, would cause "an exceedingly great many [to] stumble."

The angel then revealed to Nephi God's plan to alleviate the stumbling. Jesus would manifest himself and minister to the seed of Nephi. The Nephites would write "many things" which would be "plain and precious," the record would be "hid up," and it would come forth unto the Gentiles by the gift and power of the Lamb. The second record (the Book of Mormon) would therefore restore plain and precious gospel truths which had been taken from the first record the Bible. (1 Nephi 13:24–40.)

Nephi's revelation has significant application for Latter-day Saints. Failure to incorporate the gospel plainness of the Book of Mormon into the study of the Bible is failure to understand one of the central purposes of the

Book of Mormon's existence. For example, in making a search from the Gospel of Matthew through the book of Revelation, I found sixty-two passages that make direct reference to Jesus' sacrifice for the remission of sin. Of the sixty-two passages, fifty-six refer to the Atonement or the effects of the Atonement but are not sustained with a definitive explanation; in other words, no scriptural passage precedes or follows to explain the doctrine. In making a contrast between the New Testament and the Book of Mormon messages on the Atonement, one will find that the New Testament is largely descriptive of the atoning *mission* but not descriptive of the atoning *doctrine*. The New Testament tells us that there *was* an atonement for sin; the Nephite record explains with clarity and depth *why* one was necessary.

Having all the pieces of the gospel puzzle enriches testimony and thus strengthens personal commitment to stay true to the cause. The Book of Mormon was sent to fortify, expand, clarify, and correct the biblical text. Indeed, the Book of Mormon is another testament of Jesus Christ.

Partaking of the Sacrament

Partaking of the sacrament gives us a weekly opportunity to evaluate our lives and commit ourselves to righteous living. The Sabbath closes, and Monday we are again about the business of daily life. Between Sabbaths we make mistakes and perhaps stray from the center section of the straight and narrow path we are expected to walk. The Sabbath comes and again we evaluate, repent, partake of the sacrament, renew our covenants, and readjust our position on the path. Week after week we follow this pattern.

Some sins require confession to priesthood authority. Often in such cases the individual is restricted from partaking of the sacrament for a period of time until he shows sufficient change of attitude and behavior. When a Church member is excommunicated the requirement is rebaptism before he has the privilege once again of partaking of the sacrament.

Rarely do people deviate "overnight" from the path of righteousness to being restricted from the sacrament. Usually the course downward is slow, the "greater sin" being preceded by "lesser sins" that have been left unchecked. The Lord, in his wisdom, has given us the opportunity to take the sacrament every week. The key, therefore, is never to be more than a week away in worthiness from partaking of the sacrament. Sometimes we have a hard time conceiving of soul-saving righteousness over a lifetime of temptation and trial. We all, however, understand Monday-to-Sunday living. If we were to live another fifty years, we would have about 2,600 Sundays in which to take the sacrament and thus analyze ourselves and make the necessary adjustments to stay on course. Looking at it in this way, life then consists of taking 2,600 steps to heaven. Our focus is not on instant perfection in all areas of our life, but on incremental righteousness. With faith, we say at baptism that we commit ourselves to a lifetime of righteousness. Not knowing the future, we "hope for things which are not seen" (Alma 32:21).

However, this faith is transformed into a confident knowledge in our ability to commit ourselves to a week of righteousness. This is because weeks are plannable, see-able, do-able, elements of time—achieving success inspires more success. As we take weekly steps toward the celestial kingdom our confidence grows in our ability to keep taking these steps. Habits having been formed, all we need to do is "keep on keeping on," following this pattern of movement.

Sincerely partaking of the sacrament also produces the kind of introspection that will prevent us from remaining on plateaus. We will not just be active in the Church, but we will also be active in the gospel. In other words, we will not just be going through the motions of discipleship or membership in the Church; rather, we will have the heart of a disciple.

Worthily partaking of the sacrament qualifies one to benefit from the Lord's promise that if we always remember him, keep his commandments, and take upon ourselves the name of Jesus Christ, we will always have his Spirit to be with us. This gift of the Spirit is given to help us achieve success in keeping our commitment. The Spirit functions during the week to strengthen, soften, instruct, warn, chasten, reward, teach, comfort, build, fortify, and remind us. If his influence diminishes as we reject his effort, it will return with renewed intensity as we examine ourselves, repent, and again partake of the sacrament.

15

Why Members Become Inactive

People separate themselves from the Church for many reasons. In some wards or branches more than 50 percent of the membership is inactive.

Enduring to the end requires both activity in the gospel and activity in the Church. There is a difference between the "gospel" and the "Church." The gospel is centered in the atoning sacrifice of Jesus Christ (see 3 Nephi 27:13–18). The Church is the organization that teaches the gospel and administers the ordinances of salvation. To be active in the gospel one performs the inward and private acts of discipleship that grow out of an understanding and appreciation of the Atonement: charity, mercy, forgiveness, service, and so on. To be active in the Church one attends the meetings, serves in callings as assigned, and participates in the various functions.

With this understanding one can see that it is possible to be active in the Church but not active in the gospel. In other words, one can appear to others to be an active member (doing the outward, "seeable" things) while in reality being quietly inactive spiritually. Yet one cannot be fully committed to the gospel and be inactive in the Church. If a person commits himself to the gospel, he must of necessity be committed to the organization that carries the gospel forth. The Pharisees of Jesus' day were a good example of a group who prided themselves in the outward evidences of Church activity, but inwardly they were spiritually dead. Jesus told them: "Woe unto you, scribes and Pharisees, hypocrites! for ye pay tithe of mint and anise and cummin, and have omitted the weightier matters of the law, judgment, mercy, and faith: these ought ye to have done, and not to leave the other undone" (Matthew 23:23).

In some instances activity in the Church gives birth to activity in the gospel. People go through or enhance the conversion process as they learn and serve in the Church. In the reverse process, when people separate themselves from the Church they have perhaps stopped growing or have died spiritually long before they physically stopped attending the meetings. It is important to understand these concepts because the command is to endure to the end in righteousness, which principle goes beyond mere attendance at the various Church services.

During a discussion in one of my Book of Mormon classes at Brigham Young University, I asked groups of students to prepare a list of reasons why people detach themselves from the Church, or become inactive, using their experience and observation in the Church, to do so. The following paragraph summarizes the responses:

Having worldly priorities; seeing bad examples from other members; having weak testimonies; blaming God for trials in life; having no testimony; having someone hurt their feelings; acquiring the wrong friends; being too lazy; having too much pride; disliking the doctrines; being discouraged; become disillusioned after joining the Church; experiencing peer pressure; having differences of opinions; giving in to temptations; feeling guilt; having different values; joining the Church for the wrong reasons; lacking support; having personal problems; fearing excommunication; feeling that other things are more fun than the Church; having an inactive family; thinking it is easier not to be active; lacking fellowship; having too much intellectual knowledge; having bad habits that are difficult to break; failing to study and pray; feeling that the commandments are too hard to keep.

Forewarned Is Forearmed

The above list is a good starting place for preplanning ways of overcoming the problems people encounter in their efforts to remain faithful. We can learn from the experiences of others who, for all the various reasons listed and perhaps many more, have dropped away either temporarily or permanently from the straight and narrow path. A wise course would be to analyze the reasons for inactivity, picture ourselves in those situations, and predetermine alternate ways to handle the problems. By so doing we would be prepared to stand firm against the opposition.

On this basis the attitude becomes how we solve the problem rather than how we can get away from the problem. Reason is allowed to operate more fully because we have filled ourselves with understanding, and the emotion of the moment thereby is lessened. Programming ourselves prior to receiving temptation also helps us escape the traps of excuse-making or affixing blame upon another. If someone offends me at church it is illogical to take my anger out on the Savior by not attending his Church. *My* problem is with the *person*. Jesus gave us many principles on how to interact with others when we are wronged personally, as well as when we are maligned or ill-treated by another.

Count the Cost of Discipleship

In speaking about the responsibility of wisely considering the commitment of discipleship, Jesus told the multitude:

> For which of you, intending to build a tower, sitteth not down first, and counteth the cost, whether he have sufficient to finish it?
>
> Lest haply, after he hath laid the foundation, and is not able to finish it, all that behold it begin to mock him,
>
> Saying, This man began to build, and was not able to finish. (Luke 14:28–30.)

Jesus then gave a second parable that portrayed the same message:

> Or what king, going to make war against another king, sitteth not down first, and consulteth whether he be able with ten thousand to meet him that cometh against him with twenty thousand?
>
> Or else, while the other is yet a great way off, he sendeth an ambassage, and desireth conditions of peace. (Luke 14:31–32.)

Jesus then summarized the message of the parables by saying:

> So likewise, whosoever he be of you that forsaketh not all that he hath, he cannot be my disciple (Luke 14:33).

At the time of baptism we are to humble ourselves before God and come forth with a broken heart and a contrite spirit. We witness before the Church that we have truly repented of our sins and are willing to take upon ourselves the name of Jesus Christ with a determination to serve him to the end (see D&C 20:37).

Nephi was a good model of determination. In response to his father's request that his sons return to Jerusalem to retrieve the brass plates, Nephi said: "I will go and do the things which the Lord hath commanded . . ." (1 Nephi 3:7). Can we suppose that Nephi had any idea what he would have to go through to achieve success in keeping his commitment to get the plates? Laban robbed him and tried to murder him, his brother beat him with a rod, and finally he had to kill Laban. He could have quit at any point, yet he chose to endure the tests that confronted him.

Similarly, at the time of baptism into the Church we are saying, "I will go and do." Our test is to endure in righteousness to the end. We have no idea of the trials or troubles that lie ahead as obstacles in our quest of achieving this goal. We walk by faith and place our trust in a loving God who is interested in our success. Our willingness to forsake all, as Jesus commands, perhaps can include forsaking the tendency to "flee" when gospel living or Church obligations become inconvenient. When we build a tower of faithfulness let the cost include the necessary substance or materials to withstand the various storms of life: mists of darkness (see 1 Nephi 8:23), shafts in the whirlwind (see Helaman 5:12), fierce winds that gather blackness (see D&C 122:7); and perhaps even the gaping of the very jaws of hell (see D&C 122:7).

Speaking of latter-day Gentiles, Nephi said: "For none of these can I hope except they shall be reconciled unto Christ, and *enter* into the narrow gate, and *walk* in the strait path which leads to life, and continue in the path until the end of the day of probation" (2 Nephi 33:9; italics added). In order to obtain eternal life we must be able to endure our walk on the path for the required distance.

16

For Time and All Eternity

There is a multitude of written material on the marriage covenant. The purpose of this chapter is to briefly restate the significance of having a helpmate in sustaining righteousness throughout life.

Temple marriage begins a partnership which secures continued support; each individual shares the goal of exaltation. The covenant enables one to make use of the "buddy system" of support. A cardinal rule of scuba diving is to always go with a friend because there are unexpected dangers that could prove fatal. As in scuba diving, the marriage partner can provide the watchful assistance needed in keeping the loved one on the right course.

Whom Shall I Marry?

The wise selection of a marriage partner is critical. Happy marriages, which require constant attention and nourishment, sweeten life and give one motivation to endure. Hardships are easier to bear when there is another who, by covenant and personal choice, is there to encour-

age and extend love. On the other hand, problem marriages can produce discouragement, contention, disappointment, and stress that can destroy even the strongest
individuals. No one enters into marriage with any guaran-
tees. Even though a couple has been sealed for time and all
eternity, that sealing can be broken through sin, rejection,
or indifference to the gospel by either spouse. Concerning
the selection of a marriage partner President Spencer W.
Kimball said:

> The greatest single factor affecting what you are going
> to be tomorrow, your activity, your attitudes, your even-
> tual destiny . . . is the one decision you make that moonlit
> night when you ask that individual to be your companion
> for life. That's the most important decision of your entire
> life! It isn't where you are going to school, or what lessons
> you are going to study, or what your major is, or how you
> are going to make your living. These, though important,
> are incidental and nothing compared with the important
> decision that you make when you ask someone to be your
> companion for eternity.[1]

The Influence of a Righteous Companion

The persistent righteousness of a spouse brings stability, confidence, and a feeling of security into the home.
When one knows through experience that his or her spouse
possesses a solid spiritual foundation, that knowledge can
act as a "road block" against temptation. Because behavior is checked by the one who is esteemed most, there is
greater resistance against decisions that would lead one
away from a gospel priority.

In my family my wife, Kristene, has provided an un-
yielding standard of gospel living. When such consistency
is demonstrated over time, one can come to rely upon the
occurence. For example, just as night will always give way
to the day, so my wife prays every morning and every
night. Next to the bed lie the scriptures and the Church
magazines—these she reads every day. This quiet consis-

tent example lights our home and gives each member of the family additional stability and strength.

It is a blessing to a marriage when each spouse can sense in the other a firm resolution to stay fixed and true to the commandments of God. In the second year of my marriage I was hired to teach seminary in Arizona. Following my graduation from BYU we loaded our old Studebaker to capacity and excitedly set out to begin our new adventure. Our biggest problem was money—we had very little of it. It was the beginning of a hot Arizona summer, and every day for three weeks I went out to look for a summer job. Since I had no luck finding employment, our food resources were diminishing and we were wondering how we would pay the rent.

Finally I found a position as an agricultural inspector. The job required work six days a week for four weeks. After accepting the position I was told that the work was scheduled Tuesday through Sunday. I went home with a speech prepared which completely justified Sunday work. Surely the "ox was in the mire" and could be pulled out after four weeks. When I told Kristene my plans to work on the Sabbath I was startled at her response: "There will be no unnecessary work on Sunday in this family." She went on with great enthusiasm in explaining her position and expressed her disappointment in me for considering "breaking the Sabbath."

I returned to work the following day to announce that I had religious obligations on Sunday and that it was impossible for me to accept a position that required Sunday employment. After I had explained my position, the person who had hired me said: "No problem. You can work Tuesday through Saturday." My testimony grew as a result of this experience, and so did my appreciation for my wife's firmness and exactness in commandment keeping.

This experience took place early in our marriage. Kristene's reaction in this situation has been a blessing over the years. Declaring and deciding upon standards early in marriage can set up checkpoints and determine proper standards that will not be transgressed later when temptations arise. In this case the issue was keeping the Sabbath, but the principle applies to all standards. Couples can firmly determine what they will and will not do. The straight and narrow path is easier to walk if we are not always redeciding what our standards are.

A Network of Support

No one is a pillar of strength all the time. The marriage covenant creates a team. When one member of the team is fatigued, the other member can lift him up. Our Heavenly Father sustains, and perhaps compensates, those who through no fault of their own go through mortality without a marriage partner. Good friendships and Church associations create a network of support for everyone from the young single adult to the elderly widow. It is easy to see the advantage of a helpmate system that offers mutual assistance in achieving shared goals.

References

Chapter 1. Enduring to the End

1. *The American Heritage Dictionary of the English Language*, William Morris, editor (New York: Houghton Mifflin Co., 1969).

Chapter 2. Understanding Life's Purpose

1. John A. Widtsoe, comp., *Discourses of Brigham Young* (Salt Lake City: Deseret Book Co., 1941), p. 345.
2. Neal A. Maxwell, "Those Seedling Saints Who Sit Before You," Church Education System Symposium, 1984, p. 2.

Chapter 3. Is It Worth It?

1. Sterling W. Sill, "To Die Well," *Ensign*, November 1976, p. 48.

Chapter 4. The Nature of the Opposition

1. Ezra Taft Benson, "The Book of Mormon is the Word of God," *Ensign*, June, 1975, p. 65 (italics added).
2. *The American Heritage Dictionary of the English Language*, William Morris, editor (New York: Houghton Mifflin Co., 1969).
3. Joseph F. Smith, *Gospel Doctrine* (Salt Lake City: Deseret Book Co., 1968), pp. 312–13.
4. Clyde J. Williams, "Securing Divine Protection: Putting on the Whole Armor of God," in *The New Testament and the Latter-day Saints* (Orem, Utah: Randall Book Co., 1987), pp. 374–75.
5. *Ibid.*, p. 373.
6. *Ibid.*, p. 373.

Chapter 5. The Power of Testimony

1. From an address by Harold B. Lee given at Brigham Young University, June 28, 1955.
2. Bruce R. McConkie, *Mormon Doctrine* (Salt Lake City: Bookcraft, 1966), p. 786.
3. Ezra Taft Benson, "The Book of Mormon—Keystone of Our Religion," *Ensign*, November 1986, p. 6.
4. Bruce R. McConkie, "What Think Ye of the Book of Mormon?" *Ensign*, November 1983, pp. 73–74.
5. C. S. Lewis, in *The Weight of Glory and Other Addresses* (New York: Macmillan, Collier Books, 1980), p. 92.
6. Spencer W. Kimball, *The Teachings of Spencer W. Kimball*, ed. Edward L. Kimball (Salt Lake City: Bookcraft, 1982), p. 57.
7. Gordon B. Hinckley, "Be Not Deceived," *Ensign*, November 1983, p. 46.
8. Letter to the Editor, "Find Me a Better Church," *Central Utah Journal*, 1982 (author's name withheld).

Chapter 6. The Sustaining Vision

1. Record in possession of author.
2. Sterling W. Sill, "To Die Well," *Ensign*, November 1976, pp. 46–47.
3. *Book of Mormon Student Manual*, second edition (Salt Lake City: The Church of Jesus Christ of Latter-day Saints, 1981), p. 523.

Chapter 7. The Holy Ghost

1. Spencer W. Kimball, *The Teachings of Spencer W. Kimball*, ed. Edward L. Kimball (Salt Lake City: Bookcraft, 1982), p. 113.
2. *Ibid.*, p. 55.
3. Blaine M. Yorgason and Brenton G. Yorgason, *Others* (Salt Lake City: Bookcraft, 1978), p. 130.
4. Clair Middlemiss, comp., *Cherished Experiences from the Writings of President David O. McKay* (Salt Lake City: Deseret Book Co., 1955), pp. 62–63.
5. F. Burton Howard, "The Gift of Knowing," *Fireside and Devotional Speeches, 1982–83* (Provo, Utah: Brigham Young University Publications, 1983), p. 47.

Chapter 9. Power Through Obedience

1. *Priests Manual, Course B* (Salt Lake City: The Church of Jesus Christ of Latter-day Saints, 1984), pp. 84–85.

Chapter 10. Decisions for Righteousness

1. Spencer W. Kimball, *The Teachings of Spencer W. Kimball*, ed. Edward L. Kimball (Salt Lake City: Bookcraft, 1982), p. 156.
2. *Ibid.*, p. 152.

Chapter 11. God Is Faithful

1. Spencer W. Kimball, *Tragedy or Destiny?* (Salt Lake City: Deseret Book Co., 1977), p. 3.

Chapter 12. Remember, Remember

1. B. West Belnap, *Faith Amid Skepticism* (Provo, Utah: Brigham Young University Publications, Adult Education and Extension Services, 1963), pp. 69–70.

Chapter 13. The Purpose of the Church

1. Bruce R. McConkie, "Jesus Christ and Him Crucified," *1976 Devotional Speeches of the Year* (Provo, Utah: Brigham Young University Press, 1977), pp. 400–401.

Chapter 14. Prayer, Scripture, Sacrament

1. Boyd K. Packer, "Teach The Scriptures" (Salt Lake City: Church Education System, 1978), p. 5.
2. Ezra Taft Benson, "The Book of Mormon—Keystone of Our Religion," *Ensign*, November 1986, p. 7.
3. *History of the Church*, 4:461.

Chapter 16. For Time and All Eternity

1. Spencer W. Kimball, *The Teachings of Spencer W. Kimball*, ed. Edward L. Kimball (Salt Lake City: Bookcraft, 1982), p. 301.

Index

– A –

Abraham, 11–12, 14
Adam and Eve, 12, 15–17
Adversity, 2, 102–7
Agency, 94, 96, 98, 106
Allegory of Zenos, 99
Alma the Elder, 23–24, 36, 122
Alma the Younger, 65, 94, 105, 112, 127
  conversion of, 108–9
  on faith, 79, 102–4
  on looking forward to Judgment Day,
    56–57
  on mortality, 13
  on the Liahona, 65–66
  on the suffering of Christ, 63–64
Amalickiah, 37–39
Amaron, 102
Ammonihah, 105
Amulek, 6, 94, 105
Anger, 28
Apathy, 29, 31
Apostasy, 120–21
Atheists, 82
Atonement, 6, 11, 15–18, 35, 64–65,
  109, 114, 118, 131, 134

– B –

Ballard, Melvin J., dream about the
  Savior, 61

Baptism, 2, 5, 8, 26, 62–63, 78, 117,
  137, 138
Baptismal covenants, 23–24, 103, 116,
  131
Belnap, B. West, 110–11
Benjamin (Nephite prophet-king), 22, 34,
  114–15
Benson, Ezra Taft, on the Book of
  Mormon, 27, 47, 128–29
  on trials, 93–94
Bible, 130–31
Birth defects, 48–50
Bishops, 84
Blessings, 93, 94
  priesthood, 15, 93, 118
Bodies, celestial, 24–25
Book of Mormon, 27, 28, 76, 82, 88,
  98–99, 101, 105, 122, 128–31
  testimony of, 46–47
Brass plates of Laban, 68, 94, 137
Brigham Young University, 7, 65, 135
Brigham Young University–Hawaii, 77,
  92, 109
Broken heart and contrite spirit, 17, 86,
  137
Brother of Jared, 94, 122

– C –

Celestial kingdom, 8, 21–22, 55, 67, 77,
  79, 96, 113

Chastity, 40–41
Children, teaching, 114, 116
Choices, 95–100
Church activity, 9, 115–19, 134–38
Church College of Hawaii, 89–91
Church donations, 116
Church inactivity, reasons for, 135–36
Church meetings, 115–16
Church records, 118
Comforter, 63–64
  See also Holy Ghost
Commandments, 74–83
Conscience, 67, 122
Conversion, 78
Converts, 117–18
Courage, 73
Covenants, baptismal, 23–24, 103, 116
  renewal of, 131–33
Cowdery, Oliver, 8, 19, 128
Creation, 15, 17, 18

– D –

Death, 7, 8, 16, 48, 91, 105
  spiritual, 16–17
Decisions, 95–100
Depression, 63, 91–93
Despair, 80
Diligence, 67
Discipleship, 136–37
Discouragement, 31, 63, 92
Divorce, 31, 63, 91
Dreams, of Lehi, 35, 98, 124–26
  of Melvin J. Ballard, 61

– E –

Enduring to the end, 2, 5–9, 17, 22, 93
Enos (son of Jacob), prayer of, 86, 109,
  112, 122
Eternal life, 24–25, 55, 61, 73, 75, 79,
  117
Eternal marriage, 22, 118, 139–42
Eternal progression, 12, 15
Exaltation, 6, 22, 139
Excommunication, 132

– F –

Faith, 2, 5, 31, 47, 58, 67–69, 73, 79–80,
  85–86, 94, 100, 102, 104, 106, 132,
  138
Fall of Adam, 12, 15–17
Family home evening, 113, 116
Fast offerings, 116
Fasting, 93, 111

Faust, John (legendary character), 60
Fear, 63
Featherstone, Vaughn J., on immorality,
  33–34
Football, 26–27, 81
Forgiveness, 65
Free agency, 94, 96, 98, 106
Friendship, 93

– G –

Garden of Eden, 12
Gift of the Holy Ghost. See Holy Ghost,
  gift of
Goals, 55–56, 59, 93
God, faithfulness of, 101–7
Godhood, 22–23
Graceland College, 90–91
Gratitude, 93
Grief, 63
Guilt, 82, 92

– H –

Happiness, 22, 98
Hawaii, 1, 46, 69
Healings, 87, 106
Health, 93
Heaven, 17, 25
Heavenly Father, 75, 81–82
Helaman (son of Alma), 65–66, 108
  stripling warriors of, 109
Hinckley, Gordon B., on persecution, 52
Holy Ghost, 47, 48, 62–73, 79, 95, 112,
  113
  gift of, 2, 5, 62–63, 86, 118
Home, 33–34
Home teaching, 113, 118
Hope, 65, 79–80
Howard, F. Burton, on inspiration, 72
Hymns, 82, 84
Hypocrisy, 89

– I –

Immorality, 31, 63
Inspiration, 68–71, 72
Integrity, 89
Intellectualism, 31
Iron rod, 124–25

– J –

Jacob (son of Lehi), 12, 17–18, 99
James, 120

Jesus Christ, 81–82, 120, 138
  atonement, 6, 11, 15–18, 35, 64–65,
    109, 114, 118, 131, 134
  building a foundation on, 34–35
  doctrine of, 2–3, 5
  endurance of, 6
  following, 97
  joint heirs with, 24
  light of, 86, 122
  Nephite ministry, 99, 130
  suffering of, 63–64
  taking name of, 133
  teachings of, 31, 32, 75, 79
  testimony of, 43, 45
John, 51
John the Baptist, 44
Joshua, 36
Journals, 107
Judgment, 16–17, 56–57
Justice, 105–7

– K –

Kimball, Heber C., on personal
    testimony, 44–45
Kimball, Spencer W., on blessings of
    testimony, 50–51
  on conscience, 67
  on faith of Nephi, 68–69
  on selection of a marriage partner, 140
  on sin, 97–98
  Tragedy or Destiny, 106
Kirtland Temple, 20
Korihor, 82

– L –

Laban, brass plates of, 68, 94, 137
Laman and Lemuel, 10–11, 58–59, 98,
    121
Lamanites, 37–39
Lamoni, 122
Law of chastity, 40
Laws of the land, 81
Lee, Harold B., on fortifying against
    temptation, 39
  on personal testimony, 44–45
Lehi, 68, 93
  dream of, 35, 98, 124–26
  obedience of family of, 82
  on opposition in all things, 12
  prayers of, 122
Lewis, C. S., on his belief in Christian-
    ity, 48
Liahona, 65–67, 70–71, 123
Liberty Jail, 15, 104

Life, purpose of, 2, 10–19, 47
Light of Christ, 86, 122

– M –

Manti Temple, 57
Marriage, eternal, 22, 118
  temple, 139–42
Materialism, 31
Maxwell, Neal A., on purpose of suffer-
    ing, 14–15
McConkie, Bruce R., elements of testi-
    mony listed by, 45
  on perfection, 116–17
  "What Think Ye of the Book of
    Mormon?", 47
McKay, David O., experience on rim of
    volcano, 69
Meditation, 128
Mexico, 111
Miracle of feeding the five thousand,
    42–43
Missionaries, 69–70
Missionary work, 76–77
Mormon, 26, 95–96
Moroni (Nephite military commander),
    37–39
Moroni (son of Mormon), 26, 80, 117–18,
    127
Mortality, 66–67
Moses, 36
Mosiah, 122
  sons of, 47
Mothers, 109, 111
Movies, 29–30, 33–34, 71
Music, 93

– N –

Nephi (son of Lehi), 48, 67, 98, 108,
    123, 124, 130
  brass plates obtained by, 94, 137
  broken bow of, 93
  despair overcome by, 92–93
  faith of, 68
  on building a foundation on Christ,
    34–35
  on deceptions of Satan, 27–28
  on doctrine of Christ, 2–3, 5
  on enduring to the end, 5–6
  on latter-day Gentiles, 138
  on murmuring of Laman and Lemuel,
    10–11
  on pride, 31
  on righteousness of Nephites, 35
  on walking in the strait path, 8

perception of the wilderness, 58
prayers of, 122
Nephite church, 117–18
Nephite twelve, 8
Nephites, 31, 32, 35, 99, 130
New Testament, 131
Noah (Old Testament prophet), 48

– O –

Obedience, 2, 5, 30, 35, 36, 74–83,
    84–86, 91, 107
Opposition, 12, 16
Ordinances, 18
Others (book), 69

– P –

Packer, Boyd K., on scriptures, 126–27
Parents, 29, 112
Patience, 5, 56, 104
Patriarchal blessings, 71, 118
Paul, 20, 51, 125–26
Peace, of God, 63
Perfection, 116–17
Permissiveness, 34
Persecution, 15, 44–45, 51, 54, 124, 129
Peter, 43, 51, 54
Pharisees, 135
Philosophies of men, 30, 125
Pilots, 40
Plan of salvation, 12, 16, 106
Prayer, 47, 81, 86, 91, 93, 94, 103, 113,
    120–23
    answers to, 110–11
    of Enos, 86, 109, 112, 122
Premortal life, 2, 11–12, 16
Pride, 30, 31–32, 35
Priesthood, 18, 46, 118
Priesthood blessings, 15, 93, 118
Primary, 46
Problems, 14–15, 84, 92
Procrastination, 6–7
Procreation, 23
Prophecies, 101
Prophets, 2, 18, 46, 86, 101

– R –

Rationalization, 95
Rebellion, 80
Reorganized Church of Jesus Christ of
    Latter Day Saints, 90
Repentance, 2, 5, 7, 8, 64, 137
Resurrection, 16, 23–24, 48
Revelation, 46, 120
    personal, 44, 86
Righteousness, 35–36, 95–100

– S –

Sabbath day, 77, 131, 141–42
Sacrament, 64, 116, 131–33
Sacrifice, 56
Salvation, 79
Samuel the Lamanite, 99
Satan, 26–41, 51, 73, 74–75, 60, 97–98
Scriptures, 18, 86, 101, 113, 118
    study of, 93, 113, 124–31
Sealings, 140
Selfishness, 126
Service, 93
Sill, Sterling W., on celestial bodies, 24
    on death, 59–60
    "To Die Well," 59–60
Sin, 82
Smith, Joseph, 8, 19, 44, 128
    in Liberty Jail, 15, 104
    on the Book of Mormon, 129
    on working out salvation, 117
    testimony of, 45, 51
    vision of the celestial kingdom, 20–21
Smith, Joseph F., on temptations facing
    the Church, 32
Smoking, 9
Sorrow, 48, 91–94
Spirit world, 16
Spiritual death, 16–17
Stephen, 48, 51
Stress, 63
Stripling warriors, 88–89, 109, 112
Study, 81
Suffering, 48, 64

– T –

Telestial kingdom, 96
Television, 33–34
Temple attendance, 113, 116
Temple marriage, 139–42
    See also Eternal marriage
Temptation, 64, 81, 100, 140
Terrestrial kingdom, 96
Testimony, 42–54, 129
Tithing, 113, 116
"To Die Well" (sermon), 59–60
Tragedy, 31, 91, 106
Tragedy or Destiny (book), 106
Transgression, 97–98
Trials, 13–15, 106
Tribulation, 105
Trust, in God, 68, 102, 114, 138

– U –

United States Constitution, 81
Unity, 89, 91
Unrighteous dominion, 80

– V –

Violence, 63
Visiting teachers, 118
Volleyball, 89, 109–10

– W –

War, 36, 64
Waters of Mormon, 23
Wealth, 32
"What Think Ye of the Book of
    Mormon?" (sermon), 47
Whitmer, David, 128

Williams, Clyde J., on immorality, 33
Wisdom, 81
Word of Wisdom, 113

– Y –

Yorgason, Blaine and Brenton, *Others*, 69
Young, Brigham, on trials, 13–14

– Z –

Zenos, allegory of, 99
Zerahemnah, 37–39
Zoramites, 79, 121, 127